Home–School

l

David Fulton Pul
London

David Fulton Publishers Ltd
2 Barbon Close, London WC1N 3JX

First published in Great Britain by David Fulton Publishers 1997

Note: The right of John Bastiani to be identified as the editor of this work has been asserted by him in accordance with the Copyright, Designs and Patents Act 1988.

Copyright © David Fulton Publishers

British Library Cataloguing in Publication Data

A catalogue record for this book is available from the British Library

ISBN 1-85346-428-7

Typeset by Textype Typesetters, Cambridge
Printed in Great Britain by the Cromwell Press Ltd., Melksham

Contents

Acknowledgements

To all the committed and very professional Section 11 staff I have worked with around the country. And to the parents, families, governors and pupils of their schools.

To Diana West, for her continuing encouragement, good advice and practical support – and for putting up with me!

Contributors

Perveen Ahmad, Avrille Oxley McCann and Christine Plackett have worked together on Section 11 funded projects in Cleveland since 1989. Perveen is the co-ordinator of the current project for Raising Pupil Achievement in the newly formed boroughs of Middlesborough, Stockton and Hartlepool. Avrille and Chris are involved in the same project, working in both primary and secondary schools in Middlesborough.

John Bastiani is a freelance consultant on home–school matters who has written extensively on the subject. He has recently been associated with a wide range of both mainstream and specially funded programmes and activities in schools, LEAs and national projects, throughout the UK and in other countries. John is currently running a part-time MA in Home–School Relations at Nottingham Trent University and is co-ordinator of the National Home–School Development Group.

Beverley Crooks is an educationalist and a researcher. She has taught in both primary and secondary schools in Britain and in Zimbabwe. Her research interests include language and power and she is currently researching language between home and school. She is head of the Schools and Parents Curriculum Project in the Borough of Kensington and Chelsea, and former head of the Education Liaison Service.

Latika Davis and Rachel Evans – Latika is a bilingual black teacher who is the mother of two dual-heritage daughters. Rachel has wide experience of work within social services and educational environments. She is a white single parent of two dual-heritage children. In writing their chapter for this book they have, therefore, been able to draw on their own experiences as both professionals and parents in Coventry.

Anna Ferris has taught in primary schools as a class teacher and EAL teacher. She has taught in London and Tanzania, where she worked towards becoming bilingual. She is currently Early Years and Infant Section 11 Project Co-ordinator in Hackney.

Elizabeth Jordan and Pat Holmes – Elizabeth is a lecturer in special needs and learning difficulties at Moray House, Edinburgh. She runs the Scottish Traveller Education Project, funded by the Scottish Office Education Department to promote Travellers' needs in education. Pat Holmes is Co-ordinator of West Midlands Consortium Education Service for

Travelling Children, a consortium covering LEAs and some thirty schools. She has extensive experience in promoting inter-professional team-work and home–school links in order to achieve equality of opportunity for Travellers in schools. Both are active in EC-funded projects focusing on team approaches to education for Travelling communities.

Sheila Karran started teaching in 1965 in primary, then secondary and special schools. From 1975 to 1992 she worked with Coventry's Community Education Project as an education visitor, home–school officer and advisory teacher. Since 1992 she has been leader of the Home School Links Team with the Minority Group Support Service in Coventry.

Alwyn Morgan and Jeremy Richardson – Alwyn taught in Leicestershire before moving to Clwyd as a community tutor in a secondary school and later as the community education co-ordinator for the LEA. For the past eight years he has worked across Humberside and further afield encouraging and supporting home–school liaison strategies. A substantial training programme and inter-agency collaboration are key elements of his work. Jeremy has worked overseas with VSO and run courses for teachers planning to work in developing countries. He is also a co-author of a teachers' resource book on this subject. He has taught in London and in various secondary schools in West Yorkshire. He is currently the co-ordinator of mathematics and IT at Primrose High School in Leeds.

Sushma Rani Puri qualified as an industrial chemist, but changed direction to train as a science teacher. After spells in both education and medical research she became a home–school liaison specialist in 1989. She is currently the Section 11 school and community development co-ordinator for the Bradford LEA.

Jill Rutter is an education officer with the Refugee Council and is also a research officer with the Refugee Education Initiative which is based at the London University Institute of Education.

Alison Shilela, who is the co-ordinator of this chapter, is a team manager of the Cambridgeshire Multicultural Education Service based in Peterborough. **Susie Hall** is the manager of the Cambridgeshire Multicultural Education Service. **Christine Corkhill**, **Doreen Medcraft** and **Bethan Rees** are all language and curriculum development teachers. Christine and Doreen work in Peterborough primary schools and Bethan works in secondary schools in Cambridge. **Naseer Sethi** and **Mehbubar** are home–school liaison officers based in Peterborough and Cambridge respectively.

Raymonde Sneddon is a senior lecturer at the University of East London who was a teacher in Hackney for seventeen years, specialising in working with bilingual children and their families. She is currently researching the role of community groups in supporting the education of bilingual children.

Margaret Wood has been involved in Traveller education since the early 1970s. After sixteen years as a languages teacher she joined the newly formed Cambridgeshire County Team for Traveller Education in 1988. She is a member of various Traveller organisations and serves on the executive committee of the Advisory Council for the Education of Romanies and other Travellers (ACERT).

Home and School – A working Alliance

This Series, edited by *John Bastiani* and *Sheila Wolfendale*, brings together wide-ranging contributions which

* are written from both professional and parental viewpoints
* offer an assessment of what has been achieved
* explore a number of problematic issues and experiences
* illustrate developments that are beginning to take shape

It will appeal to those with a special interest in and commitment to home–school work in all its actual and potential facets

Early titles are:

Working with Parents as Partners in SEN
Eileen Gascoigne
1–85346–375–2

Home–School Work in Britain – review, reflection and development
By members of the National Home–School Development Group, edited by John Bastiani and Sheila Wolfendale
1–85346–395–7

Home–School Work in Multicultural Settings
Edited by John Bastiani
1–85346–428–7

Working with Parents of SEN Children after the Code of Practice
Edited by Sheila Wolfendale
1–85346–429–5

Linking Home and School: Partnership in Practice in Primary Education
Hugh and Jenny Waller
1–85346–482–1

Editor's Introduction

I recently had the experience of organising two very different, but equally challenging, home–school initiatives that ran alongside one another. Because I was frequently moving from one to the other, I was able to experience, at first hand, a key lesson that has stood me in good stead ever since.

In the first project, a two-year development project, 'Parents in a Learning Society', organised by the Royal Society of Arts (RSA), I worked with staff, parents and pupils in a number of schools that neatly illustrated a cross section of the English educational system as a whole. The schools catered for children of all ages, from three year olds in a nursery to eighteen-year-old students, in a wide range of social and geographical settings; they catered for children with widely differing needs and capabilities and had very different histories of, and approaches to, their work with parents, families and the wider community.

They were equally diverse in terms of their linguistic and cultural chemistry. One school, a middle school in the west country, did not have a single black or bilingual pupil – but had a significant number of children from Traveller families; in another, which was an urban primary school, Bengali-speaking children made up nearly 85 per cent of the pupil intake; yet again, in an inner-city secondary school, pupils spoke 47 different languages. I have come to learn that these points of reference provide important signposts in the landscape of cultural and linguistic diversity that are typical of contemporary Britain.

In the second initiative I was given the task, through a European Commission funded intercultural project, of establishing a practitioner network for the co-ordination, networking and development of good practice in the field of home–school liaison, specifically with minority ethnic parents and families. Since then, I have supplemented this work through talks and discussions, training days and workshops with the Section 11 services of nearly 40 LEAs around the country, with GEST-funded initiatives for both mainstream and additionally funded staff of all kinds, and in links with colleagues doing broadly comparable work in other European Union countries.

As a result of this fortunate combination of circumstances, I have had an unrivalled opportunity to learn a simple but compelling lesson. Although they have distinctive agendas and concerns and have developed rather separate traditions, in home–school liaison work, as elsewhere, mainstream schools and teachers and those who work with minorities of all kinds, have much to give to, and learn from, each other (for a fuller exploration of the concept of mainstreaming and an illustrated examination of some of its uses, see Bastiani (1996)).

In order to make this happen, however, there has to be a conscious effort to recognise, tackle and redress the current imbalance between the two areas. Home–school work in Britain is now enjoying something of a high. It's potential and significance are now widely recognised and endorsed. Parental involvement in their children's school learning is now generally accepted as being both legitimate and desirable, in terms of its tangible benefits to pupils. It also enjoys a rapidly growing and increasingly influential body of literature and research.

In home–school work with cultural and linguistic minorities, the story could not be more different! In spite of its enormous achievements in a very challenging area, this (mainly Section 11 funded) work is often unheralded, sometimes marginalised, both within staffrooms and within LEA services, and continuously lives on the knife edge of annual renewal.

This book is an attempt to remedy this situation, by raising the profile of home–school work in multicultural settings. It brings together, for the first time, a collection of accounts that illustrate a range of professional issues and practical concerns, against a background of commitment to the benefits of families and schools working together.

At the same time, the accounts collectively suggest both a wide ranging, diverse and developing body of effective practice, which is, generally, in a state of positive health. Such work is undoubtedly a tribute to the patience, commitment and quiet determination of those endeavouring to get a better deal for minority children and their families – often against all the odds and always against the background of a continuously uncertain future.

Above all, the achievements described in the following accounts do not get the wider recognition that they deserve, even among fellow colleagues in the service and within the schools and classrooms in which they occur, although there are signs that this is beginning to change. A recent OFSTED report, for example, provides a public endorsement of the value and effectiveness of Section 11 funded home–school liaison work (OFSTED 1994).

The accounts in this collection also reflect something of the current wider interest in the relationships between parents/carers and their children's schools, espoused by politicians, professionals and parents alike. Here, current developments mirror many of those in mainstream home–school work, refracted through appropriate linguistic and cultural filters. Such developments include:

- the key role of pupils in home–school work;
- the effectiveness of parents and children working together;
- making homework more effective;
- the special challenge of involving fathers;
- the need to acknowledge parents' own learning and development, etc.

Two additional problems stand out here. The first is to find ways of encouraging, and building on, the involvement of parents and families as children get older and pass through the system. Ironically, there are suggestions that some parents, often fathers (where they have extended experience of schooling in a formal system), in some ways find this easier than the subtleties of a British play and activity-based early years curriculum.

Above all, the current climate underwrites the important contribution of parental involvement for the raising of pupil achievement. Here, almost uniquely, many expectations meet. For many stakeholders, including government and many minority ethnic parents, this can be seen as a justification, as well as an appropriate starting point, and basis for, a growing relationship based on common purpose and practical co-operation. The ability to draw upon, and contribute to, home–school work in mainstream schools of all kinds, in a wide range of settings and circumstances, is complemented by the development of a distinctive repertoire of attitudes and ways of working that are appropriate to the more particular needs of working with black and bilingual parents, families and communities.

In this collection, these developments are illustrated through accounts that are very different in style and approach, from wide-angled portraits of enormously diverse and comprehensive provision, to closely observed accounts of individual children learning in home and school settings, from personal research, INSET experience and the evaluation of existing work!

Such a repertoire is often represented, somewhat simplistically, in terms of language and communication problems. This collection suggests a focus upon a process of dialogue, which leads to mutual understanding. As always, thinking and practice develop together. So while authors remind us of the importance of both cultural sensitivity and appropriate resources, in supporting home visits and outreach work, they also remind us – sometimes forcibly – of the corresponding need to recognise children's culture and out-of-school experience within the life and work of the school itself, as a necessary ingredient of effective school learning.

Although the context and organisation of this collection have been chosen to illustrate both the range of approaches in this area and some of the more recent shifts of concern and emphasis, there has been no attempt to do this in a formal and comprehensive way.

In many ways, this collection can only begin to scratch the surface and to bring together a range of accessible experience from which we can all learn and which can contribute to the development of a deeper understanding and more effective practice.

So, the book opens with an overview of home–school work with minority ethnic parents and families, which explores both its distinctive concerns and its relationships with work in mainstream schools. This is followed by two chapters which illustrate the range and scope of home–school practice in primary and secondary schools against two, contrasting, local education authority backgrounds.

These are followed by several, very different, accounts where the common theme is provided by the need to bring children's learning – in school and at home – to bear upon one another more productively. The next group of contributions juxtapose work with less familiar, sharply contrasting, groups whose real needs are only just becoming clear. These are followed by two chapters which illustrate, in their different ways, some of the benefits for all concerned, of recognising, and responding to, parents' own learning and development. The collection is rounded off by a broadly focused account, which emphasises the important, and distinctive, contribution of community groups, organisations and resources to minority ethnic children's learning and educational process.

For some readers, there will, inevitably, seem to be some surprising omissions. For example, although a number of accounts are pleased to report the growing representation of minorities on school governing bodies, this important topic is not dealt with specifically. Similarly, there are no contributions which deal exclusively with the important and topical work with parents of children with special educational needs, as these are being dealt with more fully elsewhere in this series. Neither are there studies which focus upon particular linguistic and cultural communities, either long established or more recent, although there is a place for these, on another occasion.

Although contributors to this book were given a relatively open brief in defining their topics and drawing upon their experience, it has been intriguing to watch the emergence of a number of common themes and shared concerns. Unsurprisingly, particularly among contributors who are themselves members of minority ethnic groups, one's own personal and professional experiences have a key role in shaping the growth of key interests and in making contributions to the effectiveness of one's work in these areas.

Then, too, many of the accounts illustrate the importance of learning on one's feet. The difficult and challenging nature of work in this area calls for a range of difficult, higher order skills that are simply not part of the conventional training of teachers and others who work in, and with, schools. Indeed, by definition, no one has adequate knowledge, skill and experience in this area. The number of accounts that are genuinely written through collaboration (though not necessarily without problems!), is a reflection of this.

There is a key role here for both teamwork and professional learning, vividly illustrated by many of the authors: teachers, support staff, parents, children and community groups have much to give to, and learn from, each other. But this requires new attitudes and new ways of working. This is easier said than done. Neither can schools and families, however well motivated, achieve as much as they can and should, without help and support from further afield. There is, to begin with, a clear role here for government policy, backed up by an appropriate long-term commitment to adequate resources, which are based upon a wider and deeper understanding of the issues involved, of what has been achieved and what remains to be done.

This would include the need to show more commitment to the identification and dissemination of good practice. It would mean the continuation of more stable provision of appropriate levels of staffing, training and support, for all those involved. Above all, it would mean transferring the funding of Section 11 work to mainstream education budgets, and safeguarding it to ensure both a sense of the value and permanence that has been singularly lacking and which would actually encourage longer term planning and development.

The strengthening of a system of wider support for schools and families would also recognise the important contribution that LEAs can, and should, make. This applies to the contribution of the cross-borough/authority service to training and support and to the maintenance of quality, to the work in this area that can be incorporated through mainstream (including GEST) budgets and activity and through productive links across local authority departments and with the voluntary sector. Nevertheless, there is no room for complacency! In the first place, the area where race, culture and the education system meet, continues to be enormously complex, challenging and intractable. There has, for a long time, been a continuing inability and unwillingness on the part of government to recognise, let alone tackle, the deep-seated and damaging processes of racism and gross social and educational inequality.

Just as home–school work in mainstream schools has moved up the evolutionary scale, becoming a part of the work of all schools and all teachers, there is now a need for those whose work is specifically developed in multicultural settings to review what has been achieved and move forward. A major task here is to recognise the need for a more differentiated response and more varied approaches to the wide range of settings and circumstances in which this work is located and the growing range of met and unmet needs that this presents. In particular, there is now, paradoxically, an increase in both the extent and the contributions of established minorities to the educational and political life of communities and, at the same time, a dramatic increase in the spread of linguistic and cultural diversity. Here, there will continue to be inevitable tensions between our professional views of what is needed and the resources that are available.

Finally, there is still a pressing need for home–school work with minorities to be brought from the margins of school and community life, to its very heart. This is both a matter of survival and a professional imperative. There are now new and growing opportunities for this. For a variety of reasons (OFSTED inspections, school development plans, government legislation, the role of school governors, etc.), schools are now obliged to review regularly their work with parents, families and the wider community and to organise their collective efforts more systematically. For the first time, the basic ingredients are becoming available for a task that is long overdue.

6
References

Bastiani, J. (1996) 'Home School Liaison: the mainstreaming of good ideas and effective practice', in Bastiani, J. and Wolfendale, S. *Home–school Work in Britain: review, reflection and development*. London: David Fulton.

OFSTED (1994) *Educational Support for Minority Ethnic Communities*. No. 130/94/NS, pp. 5–6. London: OFSTED Publications Centre.

1 Raising the profile of home–school liaison with minority ethnic parents and families: a wider view

John Bastiani

It is now widely accepted – though not necessarily welcomed universally – that the active interest and continuing support of parents and families are crucial influences upon both the effectiveness of schools and the achievement of pupils. It goes without saying, however, that this realisation does not always get translated into clear policies and productive practice.

This deceptively simple claim, reinforced by extensive research evidence, professional experience and the sheer common sense of many teachers and parents, also has enormously wide application. For it applies to schools in all settings and circumstances, from rural schools serving scattered populations, to suburban schools and those serving inner-city districts or large municipal housing estates; also to provision for children of all ages, from a range of preschool settings, through the middle years and into secondary schools; and to schools and centres catering for a wide range of special needs and abilities.

Such a claim applies, however, with particular force and emphasis to the collection of viewpoints and experience represented in this book. For while the tangible benefits of practical co-operation between families and schools are theoretically available to everyone, in practice, as the excellent Elton Report remarked several years ago, things are not quite that simple:

> We are convinced that the vast majority of parents, regardless of social class, ethnic or cultural origin, want their children to work hard and behave well at school. We do not perceive any major divergences of interest at this fundamental level. But we do perceive a range of practical problems which can prevent active partnership developing.
>
> (DES 1989a)

This collection, then, sets out to examine that part of the home–school field that relates to the education of children from a range of minority ethnic backgrounds, with a particular emphasis on those settings where issues of access and achievement are amplified by matters of culture and language, race and religion.

The book sets out to review intention and practice, to assess what has been achieved and identify what needs to be done next. While the general literature on home–school work is flourishing, this is virtually the first time that this has been attempted. There is, therefore, much ground to be covered.

At the heart of this work lies a paradox. It has now become clear, for a variety of reasons (which include the phased reduction of special programmes such as Section 11 funding), that the only way in which this work can genuinely develop is if the wider opportunities of mainstream work with parents, and the special knowledge, skill and experience of those who have a particular responsibility for working with black and bilingual parents, carers and families can be brought productively to bear upon one another.

It is the task of this first chapter to examine this key task against a background of changing policy and provision, the potential for sharing good ideas and practice and, significantly, the slow but inexorable spread of confidence and rising expectations of minority parents themselves.

After a brief reminder of the key ingredients in the case for family–school co-operation, this account brings together a picture of both mainstream and specially funded home–school work principally, but by no means exclusively, implemented through Section 11 support. This is followed by an examination of some of the limitations of perspective and strategy that are characteristic of this work and suggests some promising changes of emphasis and productive shifts of policy and approach.

The primary importance of families

Parents are a child's first and most important educators; families are simply the biggest influence upon children's attitudes, behaviour and achievement; children spend less than 15 per cent of their lives between birth and sixteen in school; parents and other carers are responsible for the remaining 85 per cent of children's waking time; overviews of children's language development show that, by the age of five, children have acquired 85 per cent of the language they will have as adults. (The corresponding figure for three year olds is 50 per cent.) These facts are remarkable and beg immediate and powerful questions about who is responsible for this and how such prolific learning has taken place. They also have a special force in bilingual and linguistically diverse contexts, as several contributors in this collection remind us.

There are, too, clear links between ethnicity and formal pupil achievement. Extensive research evidence, which owes a great deal to the former ILEA Research and Statistics Department, shows significant and striking correlations between cultural background and examination grades at sixteen, across the whole spectrum of achievement. Such evidence, which could be reinforced by a reintroduction of limited forms of ethnic monitoring, at all ages, shows a consistent, differentiated pattern in which some pupils are more, others less, able to benefit from the education system (ILEA 1990). This, with other evidence, suggests that the key influences will include the:

- nature and extent of parental expectations and demands;
- valuing of long-term planning and effort in terms of educational and career goals;
- the role modelling of parents as learners themselves;
- the educational resources of the home and the uses made of them;
- willingness and ability of parents to participate in their children's school experiences.

So then, parents and families[1] are powerful shapers of children's learning and development. The evidence is strong, clear and points in one direction. What is less often acknowledged is their continuing influence upon their children's attitudes, behaviour and achievement as they get older.

This is vividly illustrated in a recent federal report in the United States, which is part of the Education 2000 Initiative there. Major studies (Strong Families, Strong Schools), show that among fourteen year olds in the States (and I am confident that studies of British teenagers would show the same pattern), home factors account for no less than 90 per cent of the variation between all pupils of that age in English, maths and science. Home factors include parental expectations and demands, their monitoring of school attendance, their active interest in their children's work and their management of TV viewing and completion of homework. There are, of course, several ways of interpreting these relationships!

Pupil test scores and examination results seem to offer clear and irrefutable evidence of educational progress. There are, however, many areas of educational activity, such as attitude formation, personality growth, aspects of personal and social education, for instance, where testing learning is not appropriate, or could even be counter productive. Moreover, undue concentration on examinable activities overemphasises some things at the expense of others. In the end, this has a self-reinforcing and narrowing effect upon children's school learning.

The contribution of schools

Although family influences are crucial, schools do make a difference! Schools differ enormously in their ability to get the best out of their pupils, in ways that outweigh any differences that there are between pupils to begin with. There is now a clear and extensive body of evidence, about what makes an effective school. Such schools are, unsurprisingly, well-led, clear about what their main tasks should be and thorough in their organisation. More significantly here, they are also schools that work hard to relate effectively to their parents and others who have a primary responsibility for care and development.

What does this mean? It means that they:

- communicate with their parents in terms that make sense to them;

- provide a range of appropriate opportunities for parents to see their children's work and discuss their progress;
- help parents to provide practical encouragement and support for their children's school learning;
- create a sense of shared identity and common purpose, in which teachers, parents and pupils alike will talk about 'our' school, and which is often taken to be the core of both the idea and the practice of educational partnership.

(Bastiani 1995)

School effectiveness researches and improvement programmes tend to include schools that are racially mixed and culturally diverse as part of wider school samples and pupil populations. In a significant study, consisting only of schools in multicultural settings, Smith and Tomlinson, forcibly make a general claim that:

The most important conclusion to be drawn is that school effectiveness is an issue for racial minorities in much the same way that it is for everybody else. It is a more urgent issue for racial minorities, because they start secondary school at a substantial disadvantage. But the measures that will best promote the interests of racial minorities in [secondary] schools are the same as those that will raise the standards of [secondary] education generally.

(Smith and Tomlinson 1989)

The tangible benefits of practical co-operation: some evidence

Large numbers of studies in home–school projects, LEA initiatives and school-based reading schemes, have demonstrated the tangible and lasting benefits in involving parents in children's reading (Wolfendale and Topping 1996, Hannon and Jackson 1987). Similar claims are supportable for their progress and development in maths, often in multiethnic, culturally diverse classrooms (Curle 1993).

Studies based on parental-involvement elements of neighbourhood-based, community development projects in Coventry, showed substantial improvements in children's maths and reading. Here the gains enabled working-class children in inner-city schools, often containing significant numbers of children from minority ethnic families, to reach the above average reading levels of the middle-class children in the suburbs. Even more remarkably these gains were sustained when children moved on to secondary school (Widlake and MacLeod 1984).

Recent evidence from the National Cohort Development Studies (large-scale studies of people born in England in 1970), relate the basic skills problems of young adults to much earlier problems. 'The evidence shows ... that teachers and parents working in combination to help primary school children with their reading and numeracy will make a strong contribution to preventing failure' (Bynner and Steedman 1995).

Well-known studies by Headstart and High Scope have demonstrated, in work that has been replicated in other countries, that involving parents as co-educators in their children's learning and development also has a wide range of long-term benefits (Ball 1994). More recently, similar patterns have been shown in long- term studies, based on the Strathclyde Partnership Projects (Hall *et al.* 1993).

There is, then, a great deal of cumulative evidence which is consistent, generalisable across broad populations and pointing in one direction, captured in this quotation from an overview of the social factors affecting children's learning. It underlines the case for, and benefits of, home–school co-operation in terms of tangible and lasting gains in pupil achievement. This applies in all types of institutions, across the age ranges of pupils and in a growing number of countries around the world. 'If we are serious about wanting to try to equalize opportunities for school children, we must address the issue of parental involvement, which is probably the main source of differences among the children' (Lake 1995).

Minority ethnic families and their children's schooling

A wide-angled view

Many of the issues and problems explored in this collection are common to educational systems throughout the European Union and further afield. A typical agenda, embodying the shared concerns of member governments, professional bodies and parent organisations, would need to acknowledge:

- the problems of long-term urbanisation and the continuing need for renewal and development in our cities;
- issues of migration and settlement, shaped by economic change and political instability and exacerbated by racism;
- deep-seated inequalities of educational access and achievement and their consequences for pupil careers.

The real force of such an agenda, for many of the children and families referred to in the accounts in this book, is that its combined effects are expressed, often vividly, as part of their everyday lives. Sometimes this calls for a new mindset involving cross-cultural differences such as the following observation, suggesting that children living in the large cities of different countries, have more in common with each other, than with children living in rural settings within their own countries. (The interchangeability of educational materials in languages such as Chinese, Arabic and Urdu would be a practical illustration of the same issue.)

> Cultural diversity is now the rule in the major cities of the Union. It has been concluded from this that in many ways the educational situation of a pupil in Rotterdam may have more in common with that of a pupil in Berlin or London

than with that of a pupil in a rural Dutch province. This observation points to new prospects for exchanges of experience and information between Member States.

(Commission of the European Communities 1994)

More depressingly, newspapers from other countries also report increasingly similar problems and responses, such as the polarisation of school populations along racial lines as a result of parental choice or the inevitable tensions between schools, families and communities as a response to matters relating to religious education, school dress, pupil achievement and behaviour.

This is countered, to some extent, by attempts to promote positive initiatives and counter action. The European Commission, for example, has extensively supported intercultural, refugee and Traveller education; the European Parents' Association has organised conferences and the sharing of ideas and experience in the field of migrant education.[2]

Recent experience suggests that both the genuineness of commitment at the political level and the effectiveness of educational effort are inconsistent and uneven. There is, however, plenty of scope to share ideas and experience in working with mobile populations and culturally diverse communities. Britain has both much to offer and important lessons to learn!

The British context

In Britain, the Section 11 programme is the only large funded programme targeted at the needs of minority ethnic groups. For the benefit of those not familiar with the British scene, this is a mixture of government funding (derived from the Home Office, which is responsible for immigration and asylum, not education), topped up by educational funds raised through a mixture of national and local taxation. It applies to England: other parts of the UK have their own, much smaller scale, alternative arrangements.

Section 11 funding has always been officially located with an ideology of equality and opportunity.

The Government's aim for Section 11 funding in education is that it should be used to remove barriers to true equality of educational opportunity for ethnic minority groups, where mainstream programmes alone are not sufficient to remove these barriers. The education service needs to equip ethnic minority groups with the knowledge, skills and understanding they require to participate fully and on equal terms in all aspects of British life while maintaining their own cultural identity.

(Home Office quoted by Bagley 1992)

The discrepancies between the resounding political rhetoric and the policies and budgets linked to this have been well chronicled elsewhere:

Family–school links have always been an important feature of Section 11 provision and practice. However, in recent years the considerable achievements of work with pupils from minority backgrounds have been increasingly countered by contradictory ideology and political counterpressure, in several areas.

(Bagley 1992)

Firstly there has been the planned reduction and phased withdrawal not only of Section 11 funding, but also of most funded activity to tackle social and educational disadvantage. Increasingly, schools are being funded solely on the basis of the number and age of their pupils.

Secondly, there has been an increase, associated with the politics of the right, of a strident reassertion of nationalistic values, exemplified in narrowly Christian views of religion, the dominance of standard English and traditional views of British history and culture. These have been reinforced through government-influenced curriculum organisations, the tabloid press and the cumulative effects of parental choice, which increasingly polarises school intakes in terms of race and social background.

While a considerable amount of Section 11 funded work survives (at the time of writing), its future is uncertain, and its focus progressively limited through a succession of changes of definition and shifts in the basic ground rules. The overall consequence has been for it to be ever more narrowly defined in terms of language support for pupil learning, through the medium of English, in mainstream classrooms. While Section 11 is the biggest, it is not the only funded programme which addresses the needs of ethnic minority pupils and their families. The following list summarises current schemes that offer provision, in varying degrees, for home–school liaison work with minority families and groups.

The organisation of Section 11 home–school liaison work

Readers of this book who have worked in the Section 11 service or who have worked in more than one LEA will have inevitably experienced the reorganisation and redefinition of their work, probably several times! This includes the ways in which the contracts and workloads of teachers, bilingual assistants, nursery nurses and others have been redefined and their efforts co-ordinated.

Section 11 funded work has always included a recognition of the need:

to strengthen ties between schools and the parents of ethnic minority pupils, whose ties are hard to establish because of parents' lack of English or because of cultural or social factors, so as to enable parents to become more fully involved in the education of their children and in the work of the schools.

(Home Office 1990)

This has usually been defined in terms of tackling the special problems

Table 1.1 Additionally funded programmes and initiatives

● Section 11 funding	Home Office	Increasingly narrow focus on language support work
● Section 210	Home Office	Work with Travellers and refugee families
● Urban Renewal and Development	Department of Environment, Joint Funding	Single Regeneration Budget/City Challenge/Urban Programme (Scotland)
● GEST Programme (Grants for Educational Support and Training)	DfEE	● Raising pupil standards in inner-city schools ● Working with bilingual pupils in mainsteam classes ● Attendance: truancy projects
● Improving Schools Initiative	DfEE/Scottish Education Department	Based on effective schools research
● Intercultural Education Projects	European Commission	(Increasingly) narrow focus on language support and development
● Mixed funding from public/private/voluntary sectors	● Education 2000 ● Department of Health/ Department of Social Security/churches, etc.	HELP (Home Early Learning Project–Leeds); Parenting Education Programmes
● Family Literacy Programme	Basic Skills Agency	Mixture of major/small scale initiatives

that are likely to arise and its formal evaluation (required in the regular collection of statistics for the Home Office Monitoring Unit) is defined in terms of increased numbers of home visits and the growth of participation in school-based events and activities. At its best, this can be seen as an unnecessary limitation on the scope and effectiveness of such work. At worst, it can be reduced to being seen as a form of cultural and linguistic first aid!

This section briefly explores some of the more obvious differences of strategy and organisation between different LEAs. This is not so much in the spirit of searching for a perfect solution – there isn't one! – but more in terms of the lessons that can be learned from such comparisons. These are, interestingly, comparisons that are seldom made, and provide yet another example of the low profile that home–school liaison work has had both within Section 11 funded work itself and within the education service as a whole.

School-based versus service-based?

In school-based posts, home–school liaison staff are targeted towards schools with the biggest or most obvious needs. School-based staff are, in theory at least, well placed to be knowledgeable about and responsive towards the particular needs and circumstances of individual schools and the way they go about their work. This can enable them to seize opportunities to locate their efforts closer to the heart of mainstream activities (in information for new parents, through the reporting system, at staff meetings, in the review of policies, etc.).

Service-based approaches claim to provide more flexible distribution of specialist knowledge, skill and experience over a larger number of schools. They also enable greater access to service-wide opportunities for the sharing of ideas and experience through training and professional development, for working with other agencies and departments, for example adult and community education, and for joint facilities, for example translation and interpretation services.

Some LEAs claim to have 'the best of both worlds' with neighbourhood-based teams working in, and with, clusters of local schools. This combines, in theory at least, the benefits of using specialist experience across a number of schools with, those of close familiarity with and extra resources for, particular schools and staff. It also offers the prospect of supporting continuity of transfer from primary to secondary school. In spite of the evidence, quoted earlier, which clearly shows the need for the continuing support of pupils and their families as they get older, most Section 11 funded work is targeted at primary schools. There are, of course, interesting exceptions, clearly represented in this book.

School/service-based comparisons are also bound up, inevitably, with the wider discussion about the role of LEAs and their achievements in contributing to the effective management of resources and in the provision of an infrastructure of professional support and development. The view taken here is that LEAs have, on the whole, made a vital and positive contribution, and should continue to do so.

A service-based approach – support for parents

- advocacy and individual case work undertaken by staff not based in schools;
- enabling parents to become more involved in schools, in the classroom, on governing bodies;
- information for parents, through leaflets, translation of letters and interpreting at parents meetings, etc.;
- home visits, by staff not attached to a school;
- parents telephone helpline, for Asian and African-Caribbean parents;
- parent education programmes in a small number of primary schools;
- community consultation and liaison.

(Multicultural Services Berkshire LEA 1995)

Specialist staffing versus general responsibility

Arguments about the merits of specialist home–school liaison posts are very old and inconclusive! In a nutshell, specialists can make outstanding contributions to the quality of a school's work with its parents through the focusing of effort and the development of appropriate skills and experience. But they can also be marginalised by colleagues who do not share their commitment or see the point of their role and contribution.

Liaison work, also by definition, runs the very real risk of falling between the two worlds. This can happen if the balance is lost. Then colleagues in the staffroom will see postholders being too much on the side of families or particular community groups, or by parents as too narrowly representing school issues and agendas. Similarly, to make working with parents a feature of all Section 11 contracts, is to embed it in the work of all staff with a special responsibility for working with black and bilingual families. But it can too readily be displaced either by a view in which language support is seen as the really important part of the job, or the pressure of other, more urgent, claims.

Predictably, this is making the case for the contribution of both specialist experience and general responsibility, if home–school liaison work is to become more than cultural elastoplast or a rather token area of activity. This, it has to be said, is in stark contrast to the case that has earlier been made about the significance of parental influence and support upon children's learning and development. It is also contradicted by researches into parental expectations and their choice of schools. This research shows that how a school acknowledges and responds to the views and wishes of parents is, increasingly, a key feature of choices that are made.

Some LEAs seem to have managed an effective compromise, by encouraging and supporting co-ordinated efforts in two areas. Firstly, there are a small number of cross-service co-ordinators who are responsible for work with minority ethnic parents and families. Their brief is to bring an extra dimension to the need to raise the profile of home–school work across the authority and ensure that the best possible use is made of effort and resources. They are a key link with community groups and organisations and are also responsible for training and professional development in this area. Such a role clearly needs to combine the ability to take the initiative in nurturing good practice with the ability to acknowledge, and be responsive to, the differing needs of individual schools and communities.

Secondly, there need to be corresponding arrangements at the school level which both ensure that there is a degree of responsibility for the particular contribution of specialist knowledge, skill and experience and the acceptance that working with parents is an important task for all schools, teachers and those who support their work. (In management terms, the posts of curriculum co-ordinators in primary schools offer a useful parallel.)

Finally, there is here, as so often in education, evidence to uphold the view that, in the last resort, underlying attitudes and positive practice are just as influential as matters of structure and organisation in determining whether or not home–school work in multicultural settings is effective.

The main roles of home–school liaison teachers are to:

- liaise between parents and schools;
- raise awareness in schools of cultural, linguistic and religious differences;
- support and advise parents on issues which affect the education of their children;
- assess pupils' competence in languages other than English;
- provide guidance for schools in planning topics;
- contribute to staff meetings when required;
- initiate positive liaison between school and home;
- encourage schools to create opportunities for the involvement of parents and members of the community in the life of the schools;
- participate in parent information meetings.

(extract from West Sussex LEA policy document for Section 11 Service 1995)

Parental involvement as a political, cultural and educational concept

The rhetoric of parental participation and involvement in their children's schooling is widely espoused by politicians from all parties, by professionals working within the education service and by parents' groups and organisations of all kinds. Unfortunately, they often mean widely differing, even contradictory, things.

In particular, there appear to be tensions of different kinds between the language and values of consumerism and parental choice, which stress the rights of parents to choose (actually, express a preference for) their children's schools within a competitive market and the language of 'partnership' which stresses common goals and shared responsibility. These issues have been explored elsewhere by the present author (Bastiani 1997).

It is also possible to point to the growth of overlap and consensus in the declared educational policies of the main political parties. This focuses upon the following common themes:

- *clarification of parents' rights and obligations* in line with their rising expectations and growing confidence;
- *provision of information* about their children's programmes of work, the organisation of teaching and learning throughout the school and changes in the education system;
- *making evidence of performance available to parents* concerning their

children's progress and, through comparative data, enabling them to compare children and schools;

• *building and strengthening accountability* through effective governing bodies and the formal inspection of schools.

(Bastiani and Doyle 1994)

As a cultural concept, too, parents and teachers alike have a wide range of views shaped by background and experience, about the nature of family and school responsibilities and the way these can, and should, relate to one another.

Clearly positioned within this wider picture is a significant number of parents who were themselves brought up in other parts of the world and in other systems. Their views about what are proper and productive relationships between families and schools will be sharply influenced by brief, or even non-existent experience of living in a schooled community or society, and experience within a system in which relationships between teachers and parents are characterised by formality and social distance.

For such parents and their families, both the rhetoric and the practice of partnership and active involvement can be problematic and intimidating, as the following quotation suggests. For many women, too, such difficulties are compounded by matters of power and identity, gender and social position.

> In some cultures the role of educators is seen as distinct and separate to the role of parenting and education may need to take some time explaining and illustrating how the child can benefit from partnership and continuity of educational experience across early years settings and home.

(Siraj-Blatchford 1994)

Finally, there is currently, within the educational service, a critical debate taking place about the nature and achievements of educational partnership itself, a recognition that much more home–school work has been school-based, one-way and on the school's terms, than was previously acknowledged (see Bastiani 1995).

This example illustrates a wider challenge. Home–school liaison work in multicultural settings raises issues of more general concern in particularly heightened ways. An exploration of the communication problems generated by cultural differences exposes the limitations of the official view that the needs of minorities are 'simply' a matter of providing translations of existing materials (e.g. Parent's Charter, Parents and the Special Needs Code of Practice).

Further analysis uncovers the more complex and challenging need to generate a genuinely two-way dialogue about educational aims, methods and relationships and about the most effective ways in which schools and families can work together. Increasingly, this means acknowledging an even greater range of complex, subtle, even individualised, configurations of language, culture and experience.

Some current issues and concerns

Home–school work in different settings

With the wisdom of hindsight, much of our work with minority ethnic parents, carers, families and communities appears to have been a rather blunt instrument, unnecessarily limited in scope and insufficiently responsive to widely differing, and changing, needs, situations and circumstances.

In the first place, such work has been defined almost entirely in terms of obstacles, problems and difficulties and not opportunities, benefits and achievements. Secondly, the focus of such work has been almost entirely in terms of comparing strategies, as a means of recognising and tackling social and educational disadvantage. Above all, however, work with black and bilingual families has underplayed, even ignored, significant differences between different settings and circumstances. While these differences have always existed, it is becoming increasingly difficult to ignore them or fail to respond in appropriate ways.

A more differentiated approach would be responsive to the:

- chemistry of particular neighbourhoods and communities, in terms of the composition of the population, its racial structure and history, the nature and length of settlement, economic changes, etc.;
- different needs and experiences of newly arrived and long-established families and groups and the kinds of support that are available;
- previous educational experience of parents and groups and the educational resources currently available;
- school's structure and organisation and its sensitivity and effectiveness in recognising and responding to differences; also the extent to which it is productive in its work with minorities and in tackling racism.

Mainstreaming good ideas and effective practice

The best way of ensuring both the survival of home–school work which is particularly responsive to the needs of minority ethnic pupils and their families, and its continuing development, is to identify ways of embedding it in the mainstream life and work of the school. This can mean a number of different and complementary things. Firstly, it would place home–school work at the very heart of the way the school collectively plans, organises and evaluates its main tasks; raising the profile of this work and those who carry it out! Secondly, it would acknowledge the contribution of people – both inside and outside the school – who have special and relevant knowledge, skill and experience and find ways of learning from them. Thirdly, it would set out to improve its efforts in this area systematically, through prioritising tasks and targeting areas of development.

Effective work in this area would need to incorporate:

- a whole-school approach characterised by the development of a shared philosophy, the co-ordination of effort and planned development, but also, see its work embedded in, and integral to,
- the work of teachers and support staff in classrooms and their growing skill in making productive links between children's in and out-of-school learning, with parents and others.

The following examples illustrate both of these elements and suggest areas where a whole-school and a classroom focus can complement each other effectively.

Developing an effective approach: two examples

At the school level

Home–school liaison in ethnically diverse areas: aims; intentions; practice

- Informing parents as fully as possible about what the school was trying to do so that parents could better understand the school's purposes and practices;
- affirming the important role that parents already play in the education of their children and suggesting ways in which they might further support their children's learning at home and in school;
- providing information on the progress of individual children and giving parents the opportunity to have regular access to teachers to discuss this if they so wished;
- enabling parents to talk about concerns which particularly affect their children's progress or capacity to learn;
- involving parents as far as possible and especially at significant stages in their children's school experience such as starting school, at transfer between schools and during selection of optional subjects in the secondary years;
- encouraging parents to play an active part in the life and work of the school in order to enhance the range of activities and experiences offered to the children and bringing parents, children and school into a mutually supportive partnership;
- enabling schools in planning the curriculum to know more about the families, their backgrounds and the communities in which they live.

(DES 1989b)

While this section has given emphasis to the importance of embedding work with black and bilingual parents and families in the life and work of the school as a whole, there are, undoubtedly, areas where there is a special need or potential for particular emphasis and effort.

At the classroom level

> Supporting young bilingual learners
>
> The following initiatives have been found to be useful in supporting young bilingual learners:
>
> - guidelines/information booklets for staff;
> - home visits before children start nursery/reception with interpreter support;
> - booklets and videos in home languages to help parents understand the curriculum;
> - adaptation of existing and development of new curriculum materials to make them accessible to bilingual children;
> - bilingual staff working with children in their home language;
> - involvement of parents in record keeping – with interpreter support.
>
> (Lally 1993)

Such areas include:

- the extra significance of initial contacts and admission arrangements for new pupils and their families;
- the need to establish the case for educational partnership between families and schools and to demonstrate some of the benefits;
- the importance of teachers becoming sensitive to, knowledgeable about and familiar with, children's cultural backgrounds and out-of-school lives;
- exploiting some of the benefits of alternative means of communication and emerging technologies e.g. audio newsletters, translation software programmes and voicetext;
- acknowledging parents' own learning and development;
- the representation of minority viewpoints on school governing bodies and in sensitive areas of school/curriculum policy making e.g. anti-racist and pupil behaviour policies, religious and sex education;
- the availability of independent information, advice, advocacy and support for parents, carers and families, in appropriate forms;
- the contribution of a range of agencies, voluntary bodies and community organisations to the support of families and their local schools.

In recent years there has been a surge of publications, which testify to the significance of home–school relations as a major educational concern and an area of academic activity. The dominant tone of much of this writing is good practice oriented and upbeat, although this has recently been criticised, with some justification, as being 'cheery and unfailingly positive' (Vincent 1996). It increasingly includes, however, both in titles and content, a more sober review of actual achievements and a more reflective assessment of some of the more intrinsic difficulties of working in this area.

While there is not the time or the space to go over this ground again, there are several points that can act as navigational aids in this chapter. The first relates to the manner and extent to which a school's work with parents, carers and families has become a key task for all schools and teachers (and all who support their work, such as bilingual assistants, nursery nurses etc.). Such a view is now generally accepted by professionals, whether they do so with enthusiasm and commitment or not! It is a response to the combined force of research evidence, cumulative professional experience and the changing expectations of parents themselves.

This is reinforced by a series of legal requirements, detailed elsewhere (Bastiani and Doyle 1994) and is increasingly embedded in the work of schools through their development plans, through specific policies that are required and through the OFSTED framework for the formal inspection of schools (OFSTED 1995).

Such an important shift – from optional extra to professional obligation – will, of course, have considerable consequences for the work of teachers. It raises issues of skill, training and confidence and increasingly requires clear, whole-school policies and a planned, consistent approach (see Alexander *et al.* 1995).

At the same time it offers the opportunity to re-examine and re-focus our efforts in relation to a number of all-too-familiar problems. These include:

- the need for a broad and varied programme to meet a wide range of needs and circumstances;
- the difficulties of communicating with parents with widely differing expectations and experience;
- the problems of finding appropriate ways of extending home–school practice as children get older and schools and families change;
- the need to reach all parents, not just the most accessible and willing partners.

Home–school work in Britain is also experiencing a considerable shift of emphasis and painful adaptation as it moves up the evolutionary scale! (see also Bastiani and Wolfendale 1996). Current initiatives, particularly those that involve wider comparisons between countries and systems elsewhere (OECD in press), suggest that, while there is certainly no room for complacency, home–school work in Britain has made real progress.

At the same time as recognising what has been attempted and what has been achieved, however, it is now necessary to think about what happens next. This can be characterised as a shift of emphasis, effort and concern, in two areas. Firstly there needs to be a movement away from problems of implementation to issues of quality and effectiveness – from 'How do we go about it?' to 'How well are we doing it?' and 'Is it working?'

There also needs to be a recognition of the shift from first to second order questions. This means a consideration of the purposes underlying parental involvement and participation and seeks to understand better what we plan to do now that we are beginning to have some success in involving parents in their children's schooling.

Such a shift, towards audit and review, reflection and development, now seems both timely and overdue. It also presents a number of golden opportunities for those of us who would like to see the work of schools become more effective in meeting the needs of minority ethnic children and their families.

Notes

1. The terms 'parents' and 'families' are here used as a brutal form of shorthand to cover enormous range and diversity of arrangements for being responsible, caring for and bringing up children and young people, that are characteristic of contemporary Britain. My own preferred point of reference is a recent *Government Household Survey* (HMSO 1994), which claims that three out of four children in British classrooms come from families that are not like the traditional family structures espoused by politicians and the tabloid press. Such a statistic includes, of course, the combined influences of single parenthood, marital breakdown and divorce, reconstituted families and, more relevant here, the impact of different cultural and religious patterns of childrearing and family life.
2. This is a term which will grate harshly upon British ears! In Eurospeak, however, it has more neutral connections, particularly in terms of the mobility of labour.

References

Alexander, T., Bastiani, J. and Beresford, E. (1995) *Home–School Policies: a practical guide*. Published by and available from JET Publications. Tel: 0115 9845960.

Bagley, C. (1992) *Back to the Future. A study of Section 11*. Slough: NFER.

Ball, C. (1994) *Start Right: the importance of early learning*. London: RSA.

Bastiani, J. (1995) *Taking a Few Risks; parents teachers and pupils, learning from each other*. London: RSA.

Bastiani, J. (1996) 'Mainstreaming Good Ideas and Effective Practice', in Bastiani, J. and and Wolfendale, S. (Eds) *Home–School Work in Britain*. London: David Fulton.

Bastiani, J. (1997, forthcoming) *Family–School Relations in Britain*. A briefing paper for a CERI 9 nation study in the 'What Works' Series. London: OECD/HMSO.

Bastiani, J. (forthcoming) *Linking Home and School*. EU 208. Block 3 Unit 3. Milton Keynes: Open University.

Bastiani, J. and Doyle, N. (1994) *Home and School: building a better partnership*. London: National Consumer Council.

Bastiani, J. and Wolfendale, S. (Eds) (1996) *Home–School Work in Britain*. London: David Fulton.

Bynner, J. and Steedman, J. (1995) *Difficulties With Basic Skills: findings from the 1970 British Cohort Study*. London: Basic Skills Agency.

Centre for Innovation and Educational Research (CERI) (in press) *What Works in*

Family–School Relations: a nine nation study. Paris: OECD Publications/HMSO.

Commission of the European Communities (1994) *Report on the Education of Migrants' Children in the European Union*. Luxembourg.

Curle, D. (1993) 'IMPACT and Cultural Diversity', in Merttens, R. and Vass, J. (Eds) *Partnerships in Maths: parents and schools*. London: Falmer Press.

DES (1989a) *Discipline in Schools*. Report of the Committee of Enquiry chaired by Lord Elton. London: HMSO.

DES (1989b) *A Survey of Parent–School Liaison in Primary and Secondary Schools Serving Ethnically Diverse Areas*. London: HMI.

DfE (1994) *Educational Support for Minority Ethnic Communities*. An OFSTED Report. London: DfE.

Hall, S., Kay, I. and Struthers, S. (1993) *The Experience of Partnership in Education: parents, professionals and children*. The Strathclyde Partnership Project. Dereham: Peter Francis.

Hannon, P. and Jackson, A. (1987) *The Belfield Reading Project: final report*. London: National Children's Bureau.

HMSO (1994) *Government Household Survey*. London: HMSO.

ILEA (1990) *Ethnic Background and Examination Results*. London Research and Statistics Branch. London: ILEA.

Lake, M. (1995) 'Who are the Children Who Fail?', in *Managing Schools Today*, September.

Lally, M. (1993) Extract from *Newsletter* No.1, Summer (DfE Intercultural Education Project – Early Years Strand).

OFSTED (1995) *Handbook for the Inspection of Schools*. London: HMSO.

Siraj-Blatchford, I. (1994) *The Early Years: laying the foundations for racial equality*. Stoke-on-Trent: Trentham Books.

Smith, D. and Tomlinson, S. (1989) *The School Effect: a study of multi-racial comprehensives*. London: Policy Studies Institute.

US Department of Education (1994) *Strong Families, Strong Schools: building community partnerships for learning*. Washington: US Department of Education.

Vincent, C. (1996) *Parents and Teachers: power and participation*. London: Falmer Press.

Widlake, P. and MacLeod, F. (1984) *Raising Standards: parental involvement programmes and the language of children*. Coventry: Community Education and Development Centre (CEDC).

Wolfendale, S. and Topping, K. (Eds) (1996) *Family Involvement in Literacy: effective partnerships in education*. London: Cassell.

2 Home–school liaison in multicultural schools in Cleveland*

Perveen Ahmad, Avrille Oxley McCann and Christine Plackett

*(Please note that as a result of re-organisation in April 1996 Cleveland County was replaced by the four Unitary Authorities of Middlesborough, Stockton, Hartlepool, Redcar and Cleveland.)

Introduction

What's in a name? Perveen Ahmad

My family was one of the first Asian families to come and live in Newcastle. When my father took me to school he had no idea what the registration system was. I have no birth certificate so the school had to write the details down as he told them. They asked for my name, Mahmooda Kosser Perveen, which was deemed too difficult to spell. As my father had no English, he could not help, so someone had the bright idea of giving me an English name.They decided to call me Sheila Ahmad. As each of my sisters was registered at school she received an English forename to replace the one that nobody could spell. Knowing no different, my father simply agreed, thinking that to disagree would prevent his daughters being registered at the local school.

When I became a teenager I decided to reassert my identity by reverting to my Asian name, Perveen Ahmad, by which I have since been known. Initially the school wondered if the change could be legally made, but my wish was accepted. To this day there are people in my home district of Newcastle who call me by my English name.

As Asian pupils were registered by their given names, schools suffered some confusion over identifying siblings as they did not share a common surname. For the sake of administrative convenience home–school liaison teachers had to agree with families that children would be registered using their given forenames and taking the father's name as the family name.

This anecdote told by Perveen Ahmad, about her experience as an early immigrant, went on to inform her practice as a home–school liaison teacher and underpins her knowledge of the now extensive Asian community in Middlesbrough which she serves in her current role as co-ordinator of the Section 11 Project: Raising Pupil Achievement.

Section 11 funded work in Cleveland

Section 11 has funded work in the primary and secondary sectors in Cleveland since 1978 when 38 different spoken languages were identified. Work was initially carried out by a team of language support teachers who were later joined by bilingual assistants, and a team of teachers for the Travelling community. A group of home–school liaison teachers, funded by the LEA since 1974, were offered some joint-funded posts, two of which form the focus for this chapter. Initially this was done through a bid to improve standards through parental involvement in two secondary and eight primary schools with high ethnic intakes. In 1995 a second project, involving three teachers and three bilingual assistants, working in five secondary and nine primary schools, focused on target children and their families in an effort to raise academic achievement.

The current project

Baseline profiles of target children were compiled with parents and class teachers in order to establish a starting point. These included levels for the National Curriculum core subjects English, maths and science as well as reading ages and social skills and were updated each half year.

The regular attendance and punctuality of targeted children was identified as an initial priority and parents were encouraged to take responsibility for both. Parents were offered special assistance to attend school-based activities, consultation events, careers and options meetings. A programme of pre-governor training and governor support was also established to encourage more ethnic minority parents to become governors. Distance learning packs were constructed with class teachers to support pupils on extended visits to Asia and project staff extended their own skills in this area through attending professional development courses. Home packs in core curriculum subjects were devised for individual children and the parents involved in supporting their child both at home and in school. In the primary school project teachers worked in classrooms with groups including the target children. Areas of difficulty were noted and home visits made to parents with appropriate recommendations and the offer of homework. In secondary schools target students were given lesson support in the core subjects. Individual monitoring with support was introduced in close liaison with subject departments and pastoral year heads. Parents have been informed of the progress of their children and encouraged to support them by attending consultation meetings and special events.

When a child was deemed to have progressed to an optimum standard of fluency in the core subjects, targeting ceased and another child was added to the list. Parent and child were praised for their endeavours and level of achievement, thus producing a 'Hawthorn Effect', so that it came to be regarded as a privilege to be part of the target group. Parents have been welcomed into schools to participate in informal adult learning pro-grammes designed to enhance their own personal development to the point where they could appreciate the value of regular attendance and punctuality. As the projects develop towards a greater focus on academic achievement, so parents are beginning to seek opportunities to enhance their own basic skills in English within the non-threatening environment of community schools.

Lessons from previous Section 11 projects

The following two sections of this chapter look in some detail at the work carried out in two schools by the home–school liaison teachers. The first records the development of good practice in a primary school and the second describes how strategies were developed in a secondary school to encourage equal access to the programme of residential visits.

Involving ethnic parents in the life of a multicultural school

In establishing an effective home–school liaison service in a multicultural area it seemed essential first to research thoroughly the cultural background of the ethnic groups while establishing an attractive programme of activities which would meet their needs and utilise their skills. Such a programme, to avoid undue expense to the school, could involve co-operation between the local further education outreach service, a variety of funding bodies and voluntary services and publicity through local Asian radio, newspapers and at venues frequented by parents, such as places of worship, the post office and community playgroup.

The first criterion was addressed by undertaking a two-year research project culminating in an MA thesis (McCann 1990). This extended our knowledge of the predominant group, the Mirpuri Punjabi-speaking Mus-lims, their motherland, homelife and mosque and the effects these had on the children's behaviour in school and the consequent needs of the parents. The findings highlighted the point that the child's attainment reflected the mother's level of education (Tizard *et al.* 1987). Consequently we added to our programme, which already included a class manned by volunteers, another English class funded by further education (FE). As demand grew this was increased again so that by 1993 there were three classes and by 1995 a second level class was added.

These classes served several purposes. They offered an opportunity for mothers to meet socially on school premises, breaking down the initial fear of going to school for the first time as many had come, as brides, from a village with no school. Mothers were taught simple reading, writing and speaking skills, often in a one-to-one situation so that eventually some could read alongside their five year olds. Publicity was mainly by word of mouth, the HSL teacher standing at the school gate each morning reminding parents in both languages what was on offer that day and extending a personal invitation to newcomers. The necessary phrases were gleaned from bilingual mums who took delight in teaching the teacher. There are no classes in this rural form of Punjabi as it does not have a written form. Many officials suggest that putting information into Urdu will reach this population, but this is not the case. Those who have been educated in Urdu have usually also learned English in their city schools and therefore are least in need of this support. The most appropriate form of communication was via bilingual mothers who would translate and pass messages on to friends and neighbours.

Another aspect of the original research was the discovery that most of our parents were either Jats – landowners, or Milliyards – vegetable growers. Evidence of this legacy was easily found in that gardens, though very small and often facing main roads, were being intensively cultivated to produce crops of spinach, coriander and garlic. Our local FE college provided us with a gardening tutor who turned out to be the head gardener at the local Botanic Centre who needed a class in order to gain his FE teaching certificate. Since gaining that he has not only continued to take the class on a voluntary basis but has also become a co-opted governor. Among other activities he encouraged the mothers to help him design an Asian garden for his centre which was duly set up and planted. Labels were made in English and Urdu ensuring much research and discussion as to names. A site visit made a grand finale to the summer term. In its second year it continued to be well attended with frequent exchange of seedlings and a weekly surgery for 'sick' plants. City Challenge are landscaping the school grounds and we hope parents will help us to maintain them. One mum has volunteered her small bare yard to a backyard garden project which will be open to local people as an example of what can be done and has been used by children as a maths and design project.

FE has also provided us with two exercise tutors per week and paid the wages of a bilingual tutor/mother who runs a very well-attended sewing class where mums make shalwar chemise under her guidance. Sewing machines are on long-term loan from a community project. Other classes provided by FE have included basic computer skills and cookery and currently a second-level class for those wishing to develop basic skills in maths and English, potentially to exam level. This class includes several who have attended English classes for a number of years and a few mums who want to keep up with children now at secondary stage.

A literacy project funded by Cleveland county loaned cameras to parents so that they could produce snaps of their child and then use these as stimuli for sentence construction with their child under the guidance of a teacher and an FE tutor. Work was printed out on computer, laminated and spirally bound into a personal book to be used by the child in the classroom and taken home at the end of the term. Parents from this group now work in the classroom in the computer corners.

A support group for parents of children with special educational needs is now in its second year and is well attended. Speakers were brought in to explain their roles from educational psychology, speech therapy, hearing and vision services, dental health and school nurse. The Section 11 project co-ordinator and teacher, Perveen Ahmad, the bilingual SEN assessor, and the City Challenge bilingual worker also attended, ensuring the parents had one-to-one explanations and support in the most appropriate language. The toy library was updated and supplemented with reading and writing exercises and worksheets to provide workpacks which were explained individually to this group of parents and changed at the end of each session.

The Community Development Project has also funded a number of courses including exercise and health matters and first aid, Mehndi hand painting, Urdu for beginners and, jointly, with the WEA and Leeds University, a weekly session with local poet Bob Beagrie and Khalida Majid, an Urdu writer, which culminated in the publication by the school of a book of parents' poems and writings. Courses supportive of the parental role were also covered by inputs from the ethnic minority dietician, a doctor speaking about breast cancer, an environmental health officer on dangers in the home and videos from the police and fire brigade.

The original preschool playgroup and toy library have been superceded by the development of a local International Centre which offers both of these facilities on a grander scale than can be attempted in school. It seemed inappropriate for school to compete in any way with local community-based projects. This new playgroup is now the main feeder source for our nursery.

This wide variety of Parent Room Courses, many in their second decade, have developed a cohort of mothers who support school outings and activities. They also ensured good attendance at in-school courses on the curriculum looking at English, maths, science, IT, music and art as a form of pre-governor training. A mother who acted as interpreter thus raising her self-esteem and offering a good role model, was paid by WEA.

Information about the school was also promoted through a series of videos dubbed in both English and Punjabi and offered on loan to families, shown to new parents and the various class groups followed by discussion on how parents can best prepare their child for and support them at school. Although only a few parents are able to read Urdu, newsletters and other notices about classes are occasionally translated by our bilingual teacher and displayed so that literate parents can translate from Urdu into Mirpuri for others. Similarly dual-language story books and worksheets are offered for home loan and distance learning packs have Urdu subtitles so that educated relatives can assist.

Weekly afternoon workshop sessions also offer the opportunity for parents to work alongside their child in an informal situation as small groups cook, sew, play number and reading games, go for a walk or improve their computer skills. Parents are also encouraged to assist at the weekly swimming sessions and on frequent trips to the library, museums and other places of interest. This overcomes the difficulty of having so many classes which are clearly targeted at ethnic minority parents as these activities provide opportunities for all parents to work together to assist their children. After fifteen years of community orientation the schools can offer a programme of two or three parent room classes a day, weekly workshops, termly parent/teacher/child conferences and open evenings which average 70 per cent attendance. The schools employ five ethnic midday assistants, with a waiting list; a bilingual teacher (one base trained); four full-time bilingual assistants; a bilingual City Challenge officer; several part-time bilinguals, some on work placement, many being ex-pupils. Three ethnic fathers have been governors and currently one father and three ethnic mothers are, including the chair of the infant school and the secretary of the junior school.

The next stage of our development as community schools is to make a concerted effort to involve more fathers in their children's education as so far only four fathers have attended the SEN support group and for a variety of reasons rarely attend classes or assist in school. The fact that we have only one male on the staff may contribute to this, though there are also cultural barriers to mixed adult classes and activities too.

Working with Asian girls in Cleveland: a combined schools Asian girls' residential visit

Unequal access to the curriculum

Although comprehensive schools with active equal opportunities policies were ostensibly offering equal access to the curriculum, when the outcomes at GCSE were analysed it was clear that some groups of students were more equal than others! At the same time teachers were becoming increasingly aware of the need to improve the way girls experienced co-education (Spender and Sarah 1980). Our own interest in equal opportunities, access and progression at post-sixteen had been developed and documented through action research (Plackett 1987) and investigation leading to an MA thesis (Plackett 1993).

The progress of our Asian girls seemed to be impeded by so-called cultural problems. For example, they were reluctant to speak out in group discussion work or take advantage of extra-curricular activities, tended to make extended visits to Pakistan during their GCSE courses and many families refused outright to allow their teenage daughters to attend the residential visits held in such high regard by the school. With the aim of raising the academic performance of all students, we began to look for ways of making access to the curriculum more equal.

The residential experience

Working with disadvantaged pupils from a diverse, but economically poor catchment area, in a school with a high percentage of pupils on free meals, the practice of using residential visits was well established. Without compromising the academic work, residentials could be used to give students a wide range of first-hand experiences; encourage social development; embrace opportunities for extra-curricular activities and give participants a chance to have some fun. The primary feeder schools were running Year 6 residential visits which were well attended by Asian pupils. When these pupils transferred to the secondary school they were not taking up the opportunity to join in the residential programme.

The school tried several approaches to remedy the situation. In an effort to boost the participation rates, the home–school liaison teacher visited the homes of the Year 7 Asian pupils, and with the help of an interpreter, informed parents of the impending trip. The aim was to canvass the views of parents about residential visits and to ask for permission for pupils to attend the forthcoming trip. A free day visit was arranged for parents to view the Centre, see the accommodation and eat a vegetarian meal prepared on site. Only three parents could be persuaded to attend the pre-visit and no Asian pupils went on the Year 7 residential.

The following year we enlisted the help of a feeder primary school prepared to loan us their bilingual assistants who would accompany our Asian girls on the residential to ensure they were looked after in accordance with their parents' wishes. Again the families were visited with this information. Two Asian girls decided to go on the trip. One missed the departure due to a family crisis and the other went as planned. We felt that the rate of progress did not reflect the effort involved. Other avenues had to be explored.

Developing work with Asian girls

Meanwhile informal contacts with students were being developed through an early morning opening session and daily lunchtime clubs. As these sessions were particularly attractive to Asian girls, who preferred to keep out of the rough and tumble of the playground, they provided the perfect opportunity to run a programme of their choice and develop a working relationship with the group. The informal network proved an invaluable means of getting the word round when something like a trip was being planned.

The combined schools Asian girls' residential, 13–15 October 1993

Planning

A group of staff representing the interests of schools, a local FE college and the careers service, held a series of meetings over several months to discuss potential TVEI (Technical and Vocational Education Initiative) projects. A mutual concern was expressed over the difficulties being experienced by agencies working with the Asian community. It was felt that some of the issues should be explored from both the black and white perspectives. A TVEI sub-committee was formed with a panel consisting of secondary teachers, Asian community workers based at the FE college, careers officers and a project co-ordinator from the Centre for Multicultural Education. All had some specific remit for working with the Asian community. One of the projects making a successful bid for finance was a combined schools residential for Asian girls. Four secondary schools, the careers service and the Centre for Multicultural Education co-operated to run the course.

The planning group proposed that the residential visit should take place within certain parameters. In order to target the funding where specific need had been identified, only Asian girls would be offered places. Supervision was to be by female staff throughout, at the express request of the parents. The visit was to be given high profile in school so as not to be seen by staff and other pupils as a minority activity. This was to be a study trip and not just a holiday. Wherever possible Asian role models were to be provided by inviting qualified professionals to act as tutors and group leaders. Included in the programme was an invitation to parents to join the girls at the centre for a meal during the course. The cost of transport for the parents' visit was included in the bid.

The chosen venue was Stainsacre Hall near Whitby, North Yorkshire, an activity centre run by the Cleveland LEA. An information leaflet for parents was prepared, translated and sent out in both English and Urdu. Dates for parents' meetings were set and publicised. In the event it was the enthusiasm of the students at the prospect of making a visit with their friends and cousins from the various schools which swayed those few parents who might otherwise have been reluctant to let their daughters attend.

The visit
The three days spent at Stainsacre proved to be a learning experience for all concerned. The programme was a mixture of activities, study units and social events. Perhaps most valuable were the informal insights gained by staff into how the girls perceived their education. Away from the constraints of school and home they could be seen, just as any group of people, to have different talents, points of view, strengths and weaknesses. By contrast, in school Asian girls tend to be perceived as the silent minority – a group without character. Three days spent working, talking, listening, making new friends, hating the food, trying out new activities and taking advice and direction from professionals within their own culture gave them the confidence to return to school as individuals.

Information for parents
An important by-product of the trip was the making of a video to be used when other visits were planned to inform Asian parents of what to expect from a school residential visit. During the visit we took photographs of all

the activities. For one working day we were joined by a video cameraman who recorded shots of the house and grounds as well as the accommodation and facilities. Video footage was also shot of girls doing formal study, informal groupwork, fieldwork and an evening activity. After the visit this material was all put together, edited, scripted and produced. The finished product was a ten-minute video, available in English and Punjabi, which showed how students are looked after on residential visits and what they are expected to do.

At the same time a parents' booklet was put together using the same source material. This was desktop published and printed out in both English and Urdu. Copies of the booklet and the video are now available for the organisers of future trips to inform parents of what is involved.

The aftermath

The aftermath for students was a visible increase in confidence. The reaction of staff back at school was summed up by a teacher who demanded to know 'What have you done to Tazeem? She never used to say a word and now I can't stop her talking!'. The experience of working in small groups with everyone taking a turn to speak and listen proved to the girls that their thoughts and comments were valid.

Students came back with ideas for further activities. They were also learning how to negotiate at home for time to carry out new interests. Over the next few months groups of Asian girls played badminton at a local sports centre, gained certificates for completing a course of ice skating lessons and helped to organise a couple of shopping trips. In school the girls joined the student council and became influential members, working to improve the school for all pupils. As the school pressed on to raise academic standards the girls, whose self-image had been shy and retiring, began to see themselves in a different light. Their attendance improved and they began to take their studies much more seriously.

Conclusion

Section 11 work in schools with ethnic minority pupils in Cleveland progressed from using social events, short courses for parents and introductory workshops on National Curriculum subjects, to a more focused approach designed to support the learning of children and raise their academic achievement.

As the work with children takes on a more academic focus, so the work with parents goes on to address their responsibilities within the educational system and develops to support their own quest for enhanced basic skills in English. The quality of communication between schools and homes depends on the levels of literacy within the community. As programmes to raise the self-esteem of members of the ethnic minority community succeed, it is hoped more will come forward to act as school governors.

Mothers have always been seen as the first point of contact in matters relating to school children. Schools have been successful in attracting mothers into educational and pupil support schemes. There is growing recognition of the need to involve fathers more closely in the day-to-day education of their children, especially since the debate on boys' under-achievement has been opened up by researchers (Phillips 1993, Salisbury and Jackson 1996).

As the projects under discussion are all short in duration, schools can no longer rely on extra staff to take responsibility for issues relating to the education of ethnic minority pupils. Where Section 11 staff have worked with parents and children so they have also worked with the staff of the project schools to raise awareness of the issues and find ways of incorporating what has been learned into mainstream practice. This may necessitate the offer of a post and time allocation for parental involvement and liaison with other agencies like adult education.

From our experience good primary practice would be most effective if it included greeting parents at the gate with updates on school events and home visits for baselining before nursery or reception and at Year 3 and Year 6. Use of taped stories and exercises for families where Mum is unable to read and provision of work packs for extended visits to homelands is recommended. Equal opportunity policies should include the phrase that 'any child retained on register is entitled to provision of work, during absences'.

A video on *Starting School* in both English and ethnic languages is invaluable for home loan and use in playgroups and parents' rooms. Where a parent room is available adult education classes in English, exercise and health and workshops on curriculum subjects, where parents can see their child at work, are supportive of good home–school relationships.

Past mistakes and failures in developing the secondary school residential programme have taught us the value of diversity both in approach and content. We now offer a variety of residentials covering outdoor pursuits, personal and social development, academic study and activity tasters. Single-sex residentials are valuable, not only for Asian students but also in working with other target groups like underachieving boys. Schools with ethnic minority pupils could well consider a co-operative approach to offering single-sex residentials for the study of geography field work to make the subject more accessible to girls. Much valuable support for work with ethnic minorities in schools is available from community-based projects and adult education provided a member of staff is allowed the time and resources to access this.

References

McCann, A. (1990) 'Culture and Behaviour: a study of Mirpuri Pakistani infant pupils', in Webb, R. (Ed.) *Practitioner Research in the Primary School*. London: Falmer Press.

Phillips, A. (1993) *The Trouble With Boys*. London: Pandora.

Plackett, C. (1987) *The Rise*. Unpublished paper on an action research experiment in group work with the young unemployed in Hartlepool.

Plackett, C. (1993) *Choices at 16 – Real or Constrained? How young people's perceptions of the future are informed by gender*. Unpublished MA thesis. University of York.

Salisbury, J. and Jackson, D. (1996) *Challenging Macho Values*. London: Falmer Press.

Spender, D. and Sarah, E. (1980) *Learning to Lose*. London: The Women's Press.

Tizard, B., Burke, J. and Farquahar, C. (1987) *Progress in the Infant School: effects of home, school, ethnicity and sex*. Papers given at British Psychological Society Conference, Sussex University.

3 Working with parents in a multicultural secondary school

Sushma Rani Puri

Home–school relations in a multicultural setting are always problematic particularly at secondary level. In this account, I am going to look at the communications and the issues that arise when a school has majority of pupils for whom English is a second language. I will include methods used by the school to improve communications in order to enhance parental involvement. Upper schools face more problems in trying to involve parents as there are complex problems which focus on parents' understanding of the educational system, their own expectations and aspirations of their children from the schools. In addition to this are the parents' own experiences or the lack of experience in formal education, either in this country or in their country of origin.

My own background

My first job with Bradford authority was with Youth and Community Education where I carried out research into the social, educational and training needs of Asian women and girls in Bradford. I set up a mothers and toddlers group and I also set up several adult education classes for women as most of them expressed a need to learn English and sewing. Other courses were also set up which would enable them to access mainstream service provision. For my mothers and toddlers group I was able to call upon one of the home–school liaison teachers that were funded through Section 11 and based in schools that served the community from which the mothers came. I was able to see some of the home–school practices that were in place and observed there were a number of initiatives for parents in the early years that impressed me. I also learnt that home–school relations are much easier to establish here as the parents bring children to school and good links can be forged.

I moved on to a post as a school and community development officer at an inner-city upper school with 85 per cent New Commonwealth pupils. This was a Section 11 funded post. The school served multiethnic, multi-faith, multiracial communities thus demonstrating true cultural and religious diversity.

The challenge in my post of home–school liaison

I felt this work was going to be a real challenge for me as it had all the problems faced by this inner-city multicultural school. These were examination results that were below local and national averages, a relatively high number of exclusions, a level of attendance by pupils lower than the local authority's average, a number of pupils on extended leave abroad and the school popular for children newly arriving into Britain for the first time. In addition to all this the school was struggling to foster links with the families. I started at this school in December 1989 and was issued a permanent contract with the local authority. I started to look into their home–school relations and made a lot of home visits in order to raise my understanding in this crucial area of work bearing in mind the scale of the problems. I was able to identify problems faced by the school, teachers and parents in building close relationships. The missing link in this activity was the contact with the home in non-crisis time. The school had realised the importance of keeping parents informed, responding to their needs and developing links. The need for linking home with school was more sharply focused with the implications of the new legislation contained in the Education Reform Act of 1988.

It was my responsibility to inform parents of changes in legislation or policies in education by the government, the local authority and at school level i.e. information about the National Curriculum, the introduction of tests at seven, eleven and fourteen for all pupils, and the introduction of the league tables. There was also an element of my post to redress the vulnerability to unemployment of the New Commonwealth pupils at post-sixteen and raise awareness of parents to training, higher and further education opportunities available to their child(ren).

Why it is important to have home–school liaison posts in multicultural schools

In the local authority's survey of the needs of New Commonwealth pupils and parents served by the schools for the Section 11 submission in 1992, home–school liaison (HSL) posts were high on the schools' priorities in addition to language development for second-language learners. Schools reported there was poor representation of parents on schools' governing bodies, poor attendance at parent consultation evenings and a lack of parental involvement generally in schools. The causes of non-involvement were not explored but it was considered extremely important to develop home–school links. The type of home–school liaison posts sought through the external funding were those of home–school liaison teachers/instructors, bilingual home–school liaison officers for the first and the middle phases, and school and community development officers for the upper phase. During the consultations with the community it became evident that there was a need for bilingual and inter-culturally skilled people who understood the problems faced by the parents in improving communications between home and school and to enhance parental involvement in order to improve the levels of achievement of the New Commonwealth pupils. The majority of HSL teachers were in the early years and monolingual English speaking. The impact of the project was hardly noticeable and they took on more of a social worker type role. The parents felt a bilingual home–school liaison person would be able to explain and communicate with them better and understand the religious, cultural and language barriers faced by them rather than a monolingual English-speaking person. A need was identified in the middle and upper schools by the parents and the community.

The source of funding for home–school liaison posts with ethnic minority families

Most of the HSL posts in this local authority are funded through Section 11 and a very few through the local education authority for work with the indigenous families. There were roughly 111 local authorities that had funding through Section 11 grants and most of them had some element of the funding for home–school liaison type activities. There are few local authorities that funded entire home–school initiatives for the benefit of the work with families through its base budget monies. Any that did undertake to finance this type of work have had to reduce these posts significantly after Local Management of Schools and delegated budgets. For example Humberside County Council had problems of underachievement and the education directorate established posts aimed at raising awareness and seeking to enhance parental involvement in their children's education, so that pupils levels of achievement are raised.

As there are continuing problems around funding through Section 11, these types of activities will disappear. Schools recognise and value the work of home–school liaison personnel but faced with budget reductions will want class teachers. It is imperative to look at resource and financial implications for home–school liaison type posts for schools and the local authorities.

What is Section 11? Implications of its changes to ethnic minority pupils

Section 11 of the Local Government Act 1966 provides for the Secretary of State to make additional grants to local authorities who, in his opinion, are required to make special provision for substantial numbers of people from the commonwealth whose language or customs differ from those of the host community. This grant is administered by the Home Office to enable ethnic minorities to access mainstream provision as cultural and language barriers exist for these communities. The time required to make newcomers fully at home in the school and community was to be an index of their success. In 1988 there was the scrutiny of Section 11 by the Home Office because after more than twenty years of funding being granted to local authorities, it was clear that the amount of monies injected had continued to rise even though the third generation was now emerging. While recommending a continuing need for specific grant provision, the scrutiny recognised that improvements in the system of grant allocation were necessary to ensure that available money was used to best effect. In 1992, for the first time, monies were to be allocated on a project basis with quantifiable objectives, performance measures and targets. The first submission on this basis was from 1 April 1992. In 1994 the government changed the rules to accommodate all ethnic minority groups' pupils/communities within the Section 11 grant.

The future of Section 11 and implications for home–school links in multicultural schools

In October 1993, The Home Secretary, John Gummer, announced Section 11, Safer Cities Project, City Challenge, Ethnic Minority grant (the funding for the Training Enterprise Councils – TECs), and other such projects would move to the Department of Environment and the allocation of grants would be dealt with at regional level. The budget set up was the Single Regeneration Budget (SRB).

The government identified Urban Priority Areas (UPAs). This caused a concern among local authorities in the UPAs whose time expiry projects were coming to an end. They did not see the connection between the curriculum access needs of second-language learners and economically generating projects. Education can contribute to economic generation as a long-term goal. Many educationalists believed that the bilingual learners started with a disadvantage and felt there should be an opportunity for equal access to the curriculum for all learners. Bradford spear-headed the campaign and was successful as £15 million was injected by the Home Office for the Section 11 grant.

In the bidding process invited by the Home Office and the SRB, research shows a marked disparity in the approval rates of projects within both grant areas for work with ethnic minority communities. The Home Office funded 78 per cent of all time expiry Section 11 bids. The SRB funded only 27 per cent of bids made for similar Section 11 projects. Bradford which was the fourth largest recipient of Section 11 grant, failed in its attempt to secure monies through the SRB for its Section 11 element of the bid, yet was successful in its submission to the Home Office.

Government policy on home–school links

The government's own intention has been to widen parental choice and entrench parental influence and control by financial delegation to schools' governing bodies as part of their responsibility for managing and running the school. In allowing schools to become grant maintained the government undertook to increase the autonomy of schools and make them more responsive to parental wishes. In doing this it has reduced the power of the local authorities and enhanced central power as grant maintained schools are funded directly from the government.

The government's interest in the role of parents in their children's education goes as far back as the publication of the Plowden Report. The report, compiled after a national survey, indicated a clear correlation between parental encouragement and regular home–school interaction and educational performance.

The Taylor committee report, entitled *A New Partnership for Our Schools* (DES 1977) had proposed the involvement of parents on school governing bodies equal to that of the LEA, teachers and the community. This sought to improve communications with parents and the rights of parents to form parent teacher associations and increase parental participation in the life of the school. Parental representation on the governing bodies and an annual governors' report to parents at a special meeting became a legal requirement from 1986.

The Parent's Charter (DES 1991) promised further parental involvement through the proposition of the 'right to know' specified in five key documents. These are listed below:

1. reports about your child;
2. regular reports from independent school inspectors;
3. a performance table for all your local schools;
4. a prospectus or brochure about individual schools;
5. an annual report from your school's governors.

This emphasis again was on the accountability of schools to parents, but it also stressed that 'teachers need your support in their efforts to help your child do the best he or she can', and there were suggested practical ways in which parents could help. In addition it pointed out to parents that they, too, had responsibilities.

The government's Citizen's Charter initiative has also led the way for education policy to be consumer orientated.

The communications problems faced by an inner-city multicultural upper school

When appointed I tried to find out about the school and its ethos. The school had a very good reception area and had the multicultural welcome signs in all the Asian languages. One of the reasons parents were reluctant to come into school was the fact they could not communicate with the monolingual receptionist. Parents were generally contacted at times of crisis and would, naturally, be anxious. The lack of necessary communication language skills heightened their anxiety. This was a reason for their reluctance to come in to school. My suggestion was that the receptionist should be bilingual so that parents who could not speak English would be at ease. This was originally given little consideration as they felt that was the precise reason of my employment. However, the school soon realised that they could achieve more by deploying me in other areas and use my valuable skills more effectively.

However, I set about my role and responsibility very seriously and professionally. Initially, most of my time was taken up in dealing with the daily crisis. I felt in addition to such reactive work, I had to carry out proactive work so that I would be better informed and have a good understanding of the problems faced by parents, teachers, pupils and the school in creating good home–school relations.

I was always informed of any parent interviews or appointments with any member of the school staff. I made sure I knew the language spoken by the parent/guardian so that necessary arrangements for an interpreter could be made. I sometimes had difficulty in finding out this basic information. The school found me an asset as I could speak four of the languages spoken by the pupils and their families. My educational background was also valued as I could speak to parents with confidence about educational matters. I was trained as an upper phase science teacher but had left teaching. My knowledge of the cultural and religious backgrounds of the pupils was useful for the staff who lacked the vital and valuable understanding that can have such a profound effect on children's happiness in the school.

I kept in close touch with families through home visits for pupils who were absent before the education welfare officer (EWO), became involved. I learnt a lot about why pupils were absent and I used to spend a lot of time explaining the effect of absenteeism on pupil's education and achievement. As my home visits were of a supportive nature, parents welcomed me. There were always a host of visits to be done in relation to behaviour, punctuality, exclusions and truancy. I encouraged pupil participation where cultural and religious grounds were the stated reasons for reluctance to participate. Alternative options were always explored with the staff and headteacher before discussions with parents. Parents' views were taken into consideration and at times the school was in fear of setting precedents and the possibility of inviting problems in the long term, if they conceded to those parents' values and beliefs which were not acceptable within the monocultural and assimilationist school values.

The weekly school newsletter was already in operation when I started. I encouraged the school to report important articles of interest to parents and the local community in the relevant community languages. I met a lot of resistance from the teacher who co-ordinated its production. I used to display the newsletter in all the places of worship and the local community centres. The headteacher was interested in the feedback I gave to the school and was very much interested in ideas and approaches to making the school more receptive, welcoming, informative and approachable to the parents.

I encouraged the headteacher and other appropriate staff to accompany me on community visits to places of religious worship, local community centres and some home visits so that they would have an understanding of their pupils' home backgrounds. This enabled them to respect and appreciate the pupils' religious and cultural values. I faced problems in encouraging teachers to accompany me on home visits as they could not imagine their territory being beyond the classroom door. Those teachers that did venture out, found pupils in overcrowded and poor housing conditions and socially disadvantaged through unacceptable poverty.

This posed a problem for the teachers who were predominately from a white, middle-class background, themselves educated within an ethnocentric view of the world. They often had difficulty in understanding values, cultures, attitudes and lifestyles different from their own. Some of the school staff had been there when the school had been re-located and changed from all white, single-sex girls' school to a co-educational all white school then becoming predominantly for New Commonwealth pupils. These members of staff faced more of a cultural shock than the New Commonwealth pupils arriving in Britain for the first time. Some of the pupils admitted into school, particularly girls, had never been to school before, never mind their lack of English. The language centres had been closed, as it was considered discriminatory to isolate children from the classes and from being taught with other ethnic minority pupils. This policy of isolating pupils for intensive English among all new arrivals was considered segregationist. Although the closure of the language centres caused more problems for the mainstream teachers this was a better move for the newly arrived pupils. Their abolition necessitated the introduction of a home–school liaison teacher.

The teachers treated all children equally and were not interested in their country of origin, or the home language of the pupil. Even after the Department for Education (DfE) introduced the monitoring of pupils' ethnic origins, teachers tended to class children born in England as British. The community profile of a school gives a clear indication of which communities have pupils who need extra support and seeks to involve parents through targeting those families. I felt that trying to make teachers realise this crucial and salient feature of community profiling was an issue as it led teachers to stereotype all ethnic minority parents as 'problems'.

Through my work, I found that parents have expectations and beliefs of the educational system and have their own reminiscent feelings and experiences of the British Raj and the colonial system of education that they themselves had experienced. It should be remembered that the schools set up in the colonies were often set up to meet the needs of the colony. Thus the value placed by parents on education beyond thirteen plus will be dependent on the colony they are from.

The majority of New Commonwealth pupils in my school were Panjabi/Urdu speakers (80 per cent of the 85 per cent school population) from Pakistan and mostly from the rural district Emirpur and more than 40 per cent not literate in their own mother tongue. Nearly 11.5 per cent of the families were from Bangladesh, the most recent community, and continuing to arrive. There were real problems with this particular community as the majority of them, like the Pakistani families, came from a rural area, Sylhet, who had no communication skills in English and were not able to read their own language. The majority of children arriving had never been to school and did not have reasonable foundations in literacy and numeracy. There were no Bangla-speaking members of staff in the school. I had to start networking with the Bangladesh community centres in order to improve the schools outreach programme to foster both formal and informal links with the families. Effective means of communications in this school tended to be through home and community visits. The Hindi, Gujerati and Panjabi/Gurmukhi speakers did not pose that many problems and a lot of these families were contactable through written communication in English or the community language. Having said that, these families had to be contacted after school as both parents tended to be in employment. The problems I have stated correlate extremely closely with the available figures about the ethnic minority families.

The school identified the following priorities:

- to improve communication between home and school, which was facing gross problems;
- to improve communication between parents and children – letters sent from school to parents could not be guaranteed to reach home via the pupils;
- to reverse the reduced educational opportunity through lack of teacher knowledge of home cultures;
- to widen the family experience of this country;
- to improve understanding of the English culture;
- to increase understanding of the educational system which itself has been undergone reform.

As a lot of my work was through home visits I realised the enormity of the problem, in particular bearing in mind the size of the school and the problems it faced in communicating through the normal written forms. Even when written communication was used, I still had to visit the families to explain and interpret the content of the letter in serious circumstances e.g. exclusion, pupils being on report, etc. This placed a lot of constraints on my time during the weeks prior to the parent consultation evenings and the follow up. I used to visit as many families as I feasibly could to find out the reason for non-attendance and to look for ways of improving our parent consultation evenings.

So the major problems faced by the upper school were in the setting up of communications with the families and the sheer size of the school i.e. 1000 plus pupils. This made the task look insurmountable. The school realised that, in order to make an impact with the families, early intervention in the pupils' problems and the involvement of parents at an early stage were crucial. I set about making contact with families, recording as much information as I could about them so that I would know the best possible means of communication with them on an individual basis. Simply sending written letters in English or in the child's own mother tongue were not working. The school needed to have a lot more understanding about the families, and teachers would not ask questions which were basic to the pupils as they felt it was intrusive. I felt I had to ask the parents whether they were literate or not and if I needed to contact them how best I could do it, i.e. a letter in English or their own community language, home visit or telephone call.

I worked very closely with the year heads who also had a teaching commitment. This meant I had very little time to spend with them. I received feedback from each year group through the year heads, as the pastoral tutors raised their concerns at the year group meetings. These were then referred to me.

In my opinion these types of posts suit a person with a lot of initiative, drive and motivation to improve links with families, as you tend to work on your own and feed information to the proper channels as required. The pastoral system in the upper schools could be made more flexible so that pastoral teachers have time to make home visits. In my school, the same pastoral tutor stayed with the pupils throughout their education there and developed a good understanding of them. The relationship with the parents improved as they were contacted and encouraged to attend consultation days. The pastoral tutors also played a vital role in encouraging pupils to bring appointment times from their parents.

Life in an upper school is very different from that in a first or middle school and the parents felt intimidated coming into school because of the set up on consultation evenings and having to see all the subject teachers. Parents were originally of the view that as teachers are responsible for the education of their children they should be left to educate them without any interference. Convincing parents took a lot of hard work but progress was made by increasing the numbers from eighteen parents out of a school roll number of 1000 to over 400 in the first year and over 700 within two years of the project.

As many ethnic minority children were leaving school with very few qualifications, parents started asking more questions. The children from the

New Commonwealth also tended to be more vulnerable to unemployment. Our parents had come to work in the textile mills which have slowly been closed leaving very high levels of unemployment among parents and their children. Over 60 per cent of the pupils' parents were unemployed, clearly demonstrating the socio-economically disadvantaged families and the community the school served. The introduction of league tables and discussions in the community about successful and unsuccessful schools enabled questions to be asked based on more public knowledge than on their own child(ren)'s underachievement.

Teachers are now under pressure from parents and the community to raise the levels of achievement of ethnic minority pupils. In particular, the educational achievements of the Pakistani, Afro-Caribbean and Bangladeshi pupils are of concern. This has been as a direct result of the publication of examination results and the league tables.

This all calls for better links with the families and improved communications between home and school, so that problems are tackled very early on in the child's education. The school has set up links with its feeder middle schools to have improved understanding of the pupils and their families through the pupils' previous school records. The new intake pupils were visited and that tended to be the first link with the family. Parents had the school diary and home work policy, etc. explained to them, and were always encouraged to contact the school. The problems of the pupils newly arriving from abroad need to be tackled and also those who go back on extended leave need to have the implications of the long breaks for the pupil's education explained to them. The reports to families should also be such that the parents can identify whether their children are achieving in line with their chronological age. Parents need reports that are free from educational jargon.

In addition to aspects of underachievement, parents also had concerns about some of the curriculum areas (about which the school cannot do very much as it is laid down by law). I made a lot of home visits when I started at the upper school. My aim was to establish what the parents wanted from the school. They expressed concerns in the following areas:

- dance, physical education and swimming;
- sex education;
- work experience placements;
- objections to their children taking part in the Alternative Curriculum;[1]
- educational visits;
- residentials away from home in mixed groups;
- discipline in the school. Parents expressed the view that the school should be a lot stricter. There was tolerance among pupils as they were treated like adults and given the chance to express their views to the student council;
- children allowed to wander out in the lunchtimes, particularly the girls.

Some of the parents' concerns are cultural and religious and at times the school is very unaccommodating to parents' wishes as it has the responsibility of delivering the curriculum and there are not very many interculturally skilled staff who could deliver a curriculum that is responsive to the religious and cultural needs of the pupils. This often poses problems in home–school links. Sometimes the format of the curriculum delivery was agreed with parents and they were encouraged to visit lessons. Teachers initially opposed the move but the headteacher was really interested in listening to parents and wanted them to appreciate the task of the school. He tried to resolve difficult situations and at times the Racial Equality Council used to get involved.

Not only were we able to foster links with parents and keep them informed, but we also had their support for improving the attainment levels of our pupils. Parents wanted the school to change its positive reporting policy and let parents know the actual grades attained by the pupils and whether they were underachieving. The school and its staff were very reluctant to concede to the parents' request. During my three years at the school, I have set up mechanisms by which parents could come into school to discuss anything in confidence with me as the first point of contact; I then refer them to the necessary channels for resolving their concerns, etc.

The school's five A–C GCSE pass results were 5 per cent in 1989, and have steadily increased to 17.5 per cent by 1995. These results indicate the outcome of keeping parents informed at every stage, realising the problems of seeking the support of parents who themselves were not in control of the situation because of their limitations to be involved. By negotiations and winning the support of the parents, the school was able to make real progress. The school provided extra study support sessions to the pupils both in school and at parents' request in the local community centres, as there were concerns expressed regarding pupils walking home alone in the winter months. I can proudly say that the school was the only one in the country to be awarded for its work in the community and parental involvement in school. This award was from the National Curriculum Council.

The school had sought to raise the parents' understanding of its own programme for pupils and parents through organising community events and festivals in which the pupils demonstrated their skills. The staff involvement in events outside school time tended to be very patchy and the organisation of such big events was left to a handful of staff.

Recommendations

Developing work with families needs to be a priority for all schools as we found our parents did not have a full understanding of the educational systems and the opportunities that are available for their children.

There needs to be a clear guideline as to who is responsible for funding the home–school links work for the ethnic minority pupils and families. There have been changes in that Section 11 has been located in the Department of Environment and authorities were invited to bid into the SRB. Looking at findings of research carried out by Julie Meakin (research fellow, University of Leeds) into the way in which monies were allocated by the regional officers to the bidders of SRB grants, clearly causes concern for local authorities with substantial numbers of communities whose first language is other than English.

The scrutiny carried out into the effectiveness and efficiency of Section 11, demonstrated a continuing need for these types of funded activities. I feel that considering the length of time that the Home Office has been administering this grant, it ought to continue to do so, since the Home Office has the experience and knowledge of the 111 local authorities.

The second logical choice, if it has to be re-located, is the Department of Education and Employment. This department will have better understanding of the educational and employment problems and the needs of the ethnic minority pupils and families.

Alternatively there should be an ethnicity factor when local authorities are allocated budgets so that authorities with substantial numbers of ethnic communities will be able to meet the needs of the families.

The local authorities ought to lead the schools in developing work in this area through providing training to the teachers/officers, setting targets, performance measures and measurable outcomes in this area of work. There should be a whole-school approach in this area and a named interculturally skilled person to co-ordinate this work at school level.

There also needs to be a cohesive communication system set up at school level, thus extending links with the feeder schools so that there is good understanding of the pupils' families and how best to communicate with them. This requires good networking and the sharing of good practice to be a prime objective.

In developing work in this area, it is important that the home–school liaison person has proper support at management level. In my case the support of the headteacher became crucial as some staff did not like my proposals. It is an area of work where the worker can be caught in the middle when there are distinct polarisations in the views of the families and the school.

Notes

1. Alternative Curriculum is when the formal lessons are suspended for a period of two weeks and pupils are allowed to take part in activities that are a natural pursuit for a child from their indigenous family. Children from ethnic minority families had limited experiences, i.e. some had never been to a seaside resort, a zoo, museums, sailing, abseiling, residential activities, etc. This is an experiential week for the pupils and they are involved in planning the two-week pro-

gramme. Pupils look forward to the Alternative Curriculum but some parents express reservations and would like formal lessons. There was a direct benefit from this programme to the pupils as it brought the pastoral group together.

References

Central Advisory Council for Education (CACE) (1967) *Children and Their Primary Schools*. (The Plowden Report). London: HMSO.

City of Bradford (1992) *Audit of Need: Section 11 Submission*. Education Department.

DES (1977) *A New Partnership for Our Schools*. (The Taylor Report). London: HMSO.

DES (1991) *You and Your Child's School: The Parent's Charter*. London: DES.

Home Office (1994) *New Grant Guidelines and Criteria for Administration*. London: Home Office.

4 Bridging the gap between home and school

Anna Ferris

I am interested in trying to trace how the range of culture, experience and parental expectation children bring from home are interrelated with their language and literacy development at school. We know that achievement is not always related to home circumstances (Tizard *et al.* 1988), but in order to succeed children need to take on the school's agenda. To do this they have to build themselves a bridge between the home and school. Now, in the 1990s, there are powerful and contradictory forces which 'cut across national boundaries, integrating and connecting communities and organisations in new time space combinations' (Hall 1992). The effects of this are various and contradictory, argues Hall, leading simultaneously to the strengthening of local identities, re-identification with traditional identities and the production of new identities. I think that this makes a difference to the way children relate to school and ultimately to their achievement, and I was looking for clues to this process and evidence of its affect on children's literacy.

I interviewed the Section 11 teacher, language post-holder and class teacher in one school to find out how they support the children's language and literacy development and their views on culture as part of learning. I interviewed parents about their views on their children's literacy development and the children themselves.

The setting

The school is in north London in an area that has long been the hub of a large Cypriot community, but in more recent years has become increasingly diverse in terms of ethnicity, religion and class. It now has a fair number of refugee families as well as a more settled population which includes families of Cypriot, Asian, African, British and Caribbean origin.

The school

The school has always responded positively to diversity and this is evident in many ways – in its staffing, in the high quality displays throughout the school which use images, artefacts, texts and ideas from many cultures, in the book provision, and in the curriculum. It is a welcoming school where parents have easy access to the building and teachers and where community languages are given space.

The families

In this chapter, I focus on two Year 2 children and their families. Mr Ahmed is from Somalia and came to Britain as a refugee with his family three years ago. They were put in bed and breakfast accommodation in another area before being housed. In Somalia he had his own business but here neither he nor his wife have paid work. There are seven children, the eldest a girl of eight years. The eldest son, Abdullah, is in Year 2.

Mrs Mohamed came from Bangladesh with her family as a teenager. She now works part time as a teacher in adult education. Her husband is a secondary school teacher, also from Bangladesh. They have two little girls and are expecting another baby. The eldest girl, Samshun, is in Year 2.

The children

I spent an afternoon with one group of bilingual children which included Samshun and Abdullah. We watched a video clip with a story about learning another language and talked about their languages. They selected photos, showing variety of literacy 'events', for discussion and lastly they showed me their 'news books' which have mainly self-chosen subjects for writing and talked about the work in it.

Samshun

Samshun had a strong sense of identity with her Bangladeshi background. For instance she said, 'I come from Bangladesh' although she has always lived in Britain, she talked about her Bengali class eagerly and confidently, and she chose pictures to talk about that reflected Islam e.g. a father and son reading the Koran. But there is some ambivalence, for while at one point she said she speaks Bengali with some of her friends, later she said she can't speak it. Her mother described the struggle between Samshun and her father over using Bengali, 'Now my husband has said she must answer in Bengali. She starts to answer and then gets stuck and says she has to finish in English'.

This apparent contradiction in her view of her own identity is echoed in her writing and drawing. There are pictures which show a full and rich family life. One shows her accompanying her mother with the baby in the buggy to her aunt's house for a family party. Another shows her on a bigger family outing to her Grandma's house. Her pictures and writing about her family identify a wide range of relatives and family activities. But many of her pictures and stories show her interacting with what she must see as a mainstream culture, as mediated through the school. There is a visit to Alexandra Palace to see the fireworks with her mother, father and sister, a Halloween party, complete with spiders and pumpkin and with curry and rice to eat. In December she writes about a traditional Christmas, 'On this Saturday I am having a Christmas party and I am having crackers and my mum made a turkey'.

The picture we get is of a culture that welds together elements of Bengali and 'mainstream' culture. Her family are part of a mainstream British culture through the clothes they wear – a mixture of Western and traditional Bengali styles, sometimes through their food, and, of course, through television. She writes about social events with Kyla, a popular girl in her class, whom she doesn't see outside school, yet she writes 'On Saturday I went to the cinema with my friend Kyla we watched Jurassic park'. She has done something similar on another day, drawing a picture which shows her swimming with Kyla and her family. Again Samshun seems to have invented a narrative about herself that places her 'in the mainstream' as she perceives it.

In the identity she has built for herself, 'coming' from Bangladesh, spending her Saturdays at a Bengali class, doesn't mean she has to speak Bengali. She talks about learning Arabic and knowing the Koran but she can also go swimming, to the movies and covet a Barbie doll. She has a keen awareness of what is going on around her. She has obviously listened carefully to and observed others' experience and found ways to claim it for herself. As the language post holder said:

> It [culture] doesn't necessarily have to go back into one little category or one little box, it could be a mixture of different cultures which all blend together and all make you the unique individual you happen to be.

The way Samshun chooses to do that is undoubtedly a lot to do with her personality. She is quite a mature six year old, expected and eager to take on responsible 'grown-up' roles in her life. Thus there is no bedtime story, she is considered by her parents to be too old and too competent for that. She enjoys opening family letters and answering the front door sometimes. She uses months and times to locate when things happen in quite an adult way e.g. Talking about her Saturday classes she says:

> Normally when 11.30 comes we do 'Al-ifata' and ... our alphabet to make Bengali. At 12.00 we finish and then we have a break time to 2.00 o'clock ... to 1.30 and then 1.30 to 3.00 we do Bengali writing and then we go home.

Samshun is clearly familiar with ideas about culture, language and learning being discussed, referring to 'my culture' and using the words 'country' and 'language' appropriately.

Samshun's relative maturity has no doubt helped her in her attainment in literacy along with the very wide experience she has had of literacy outside school. In this short session she showed knowledge about literacy for a wide range of purposes – studying, religious purposes, using newspapers to get information, family and business letters, financial affairs, shopping, reading and writing for pleasure and having her own 'office'. A great deal of her life outside school is spent on literacy-oriented activities. In my interview with her mother, she talked about the way Samshun had to do writing at home and how exacting her father was. Although her teacher complained about her lack of written output, Samshun shows that she can read and write competently in English. She has to tread the line between her father's demands that she write accurately, without spelling mistakes, and her teacher's that she write interestingly and in quantity.

Abdullah

Abdullah has a much greater task than Samshun in taking on the agenda of the school, a bigger bridge to build. I want to reflect for a moment on the enormity of Abdullah's task, for it is one that many children face and is not given enough recognition in government orders and guidelines. Abdullah has spent three years in this country. He arrived from Somalia as a four year old having travelled via Kenya first, and started school in a language he didn't know, with people whose customs he didn't know. Although now they have been settled for a while, the family are still steeped in talk about Somalia, worries about Somalia and family there. My conversation with Mr Ahmed constantly returned to these themes.

Just as important in determining Abdullah's circumstances is the material poverty of his family. Refugee families must be among the poorest in this country. With no family to help them and no accumulation of possessions to cushion them, they must rebuild their lives from nothing. This poverty affects quality of life and inevitably involves children in their parents' day-to-day struggles.

It also precludes the buying of toys, comics or costly clothes, icons that children use to build their shared culture around (as with Samshun's Barbie doll). This makes it harder still to be part of the 'mainstream', one of the lads. Abdullah's father told me how his son loves cartoons. No doubt he enjoys the stories and visual aspects, but maybe too they are an entry into a shared British culture. When asked about other speakers of Somali in the school, Abdullah listed his friends instead, a large percentage of boys from his class, 'Yes, I got ten friends in the school. I got Turan, Sekai, Erlinga, Joe, Hussain…'. These friendships are obviously very important to him, and help him feel a part of the school.

Abdullah wants very much to be part of his peer group, but he also shows a strong sense of who he is and where he is from, although he did not always have the right vocabulary to express himself. For instance, he confused 'language' and 'country' at times. However, he knew who the other speakers of his language are in school, and he tried to explain why he doesn't speak much English to his younger brothers and sisters, 'I don't teach them but my Mum and Dad they say don't talk in English … If you're Somali people you don't have to talk in English'. He seems to have taken on much of his father's concerns. His first words when I invited the children to talk about their languages were:

> I speak two languages. I speak Somali and Africa and I come from Somali and Africa, but I live in Somali … I like Somali … but I hate … those people shoot my country… They're shooting my country … I haven't got no more house … But my people are not still there, they're only ten of them dead.

He showed no signs of distress, but his pictures and stories of threat and loss underline the reality of his situation and show that for all his liveliness and sense of humour, a primary issue for him is dealing with loss and insecurity.

His first picture in the Year 2 class in September was a tiny centimetre high figure consisting only of a head and straight line for a body stands alone amid a huge page of yellow sand. He said 'I went to the seaside', when telling me about this picture. The teacher had written for him 'My sand is soft'.

Another next picture shows a house. There are two people and an animal. The teacher has written, presumably to his dictation, 'I went home with my Mum'. I asked Abdullah what the animal was, 'A wolf. A wolf was trying to eat us'. 'Good job you've got a nice big house to hide inside, isn't it?', I said. He explained how the house was no protection. 'A wolf can get in because he can blow the house.' I picked up on his apparent reference to the story of the three little pigs and said, trying to be reassuring, 'Can he? But your home is made of bricks isn't it?'

He moved on to another picture which looks like a woman with a few things around her – perhaps household possessions such as mats. 'This is an old lady … a old lady she hasn't got no house … The wolf blowed it out … But she made it from sticks. She forgot to make it from stones.' I wonder if these had been the stories in his mind when he drew his pictures. The old lady has a rather happy expression for someone who has lost her house. They were certainly in his mind that afternoon, however. Abdullah seems to have extended the allusion he made to the story of the three little pigs with 'The wolf can blow the house'. Perhaps it was my reference to his house being made of bricks that prompted him to carry the story further to the old woman. The stories, read at the end of our afternoon together, echo his talk from the beginning of the session about losing his home.

For Abdullah, this story seems to have some resonance, but what message does he get from it? The story of the three pigs tells of a house being destroyed because of the owner's silliness or laziness. His family have had their house destroyed so what does that make them? In his story the old lady 'forgot' to use stones. Could this story reinforce notions that Abdullah might have about he and his family carrying some blame for their predicament? Stories are powerful carriers of messages and join their listeners and tellers in shared understandings, a shared culture. They also provide meaningful, motivating contexts for children to develop their language (ILEA 1983). Bettelheim wrote convincingly about the power of fairy tales to teach children important lessons about life (Bettelheim 1978). He argues that in the story of the three little pigs, children learn the value of industriousness, intelligence and growing up. Yet for a child who has experienced the devastating loss of a home, is the lesson the same? As teachers we must find out what meanings children are bringing to shared cultural experiences like stories. They may not be as universal as we think.

Some writing accompanies Abdullah's picture, generally a string of letters in lines. Only the last picture has them broken into word-like sections. His teachers commented on the spindly nature of his writing and poor letter formation. For me a striking aspect of his writing was it's close resemblance to Somali.There are a large number of double letters, especially double vowels in Somali and words are often very long. Abdullah's writing reflects these characteristics. The word for Somalia is written 'Soomaaliya', and many of these letters crop up in his writing. This may not be particularly significant if he were five years old, but Abdullah has been through three years of English education, surrounded by English books, labels, signs and writing of every description. His father told me that they have no books or papers in Somali but, 'We get letters from the family ... it's in Somali but Abdullah can't read it ... Somali and English have the same alphabet so I don't think he knows the difference between English and Somali writing ...'. Yet, that small amount of writing he sees at home seems to have been a more powerful influence on Abdullah's writing than everything else he comes in contact with.

During the afternoon of group work, Abdullah pounced on opportunities to talk about his experience and aspects of his culture. He leapt on the word 'Arabic' as something he recognised. He leapt, too, on the word 'Koran' and excitedly tried to explain what he has done,

> I used to read this and I used to put on this and then I used to change ... I can read these they're hard for me ... I can read ... I can read ... when you get to know ... when ... there's a number on it and it says one two three, when I get to number ten, I can read number ten.

He was similarly enthusiastic when he got an opportunity to talk about his experience of making ink from charcoal. The open way Abdullah and the other children shared aspects of their lives with me and each other is testimony to the everyday practice of the school. The teachers have succeeded in creating an environment where children feel safe and secure enough to talk about their own lives. But Abdullah seems to need more to be able to build his bridge.

His father does not put pressure on Abdullah to become literate. He sees that as the school's function. He gives him informal religious instruction and informs him of Somali culture by telling traditional stories and talking about Somalia. Abdullah's experience of literacy has a similar kind of range as Samshun's. He has had little experience of books at home, but he has heard stories and in his three years of schooling he will have experienced many kinds of books and taken some home. His literacy development is of such concern that the school has referred him for a formal special needs assessment.

Implications for practice

When I did this study, I was struck, as always, by the uniqueness of each child's experience. Although as teachers we may generalise about communities and cultures, we know that it is a shorthand. We can see that what children do to learn and make sense of their lives is enormously complex, and that there are many ways they can get stuck. By working closely with parents, we can help children build their bridge.

Acknowledging the tensions

Bilingual families may have quite contradictory feelings about their languages, cultures and countries. For instance Mr Ahmed says 'Abdullah is in Britain now ... he doesn't know any other country ... and he doesn't have friends except in Britain. He'd like to visit Somalia of course', but he also says 'if it is stable we may decide to go back to Somalia if everything is available'. In all the families I spoke to there was a simultaneous desire for their children to fit in to English schooling and to fit in to the culture of the home, to be good in English and in the language/s of the home. Schools need to find ways to reassure parents that their children can do both successfully and they need to provide the means for that to happen. Savitsky (1994) has addressed this with her booklet for parents about bilingualism. Schools could think about addressing this through their own materials and displays for parents.

Developing strategies that build on each child's unique experience

Families differ greatly in the ways they combine the various cultures and languages in their lives. This has implications for the way teachers bring these into school. The teachers at Samshun and Abdullah's school provide an environment rich in different ways of doing things which provide an invitation for the children to share their own knowledge and experiences. The Section 11 teacher said:

Children would be encouraged to bring in and share aspects of their home ... some children would feel uncomfortable doing that so one has to create an atmosphere in the classroom that's appropriate ... initially it would have to come from us in the way we sort of set things up so they would want to do it.

Using teaching strategies that draw on parents' knowledge

Learning is closely bound up with issues of culture and identity. Gregory (1994) explores this in detail, and there are many action research projects that bear this out e.g. Brice Heath (1983), Burgess and Hardcastle (1991). Savitsky (1994) tells us about a boy called Toye who learned to read through focusing on the language of his family, Yoruba. His mother and teacher collaborated to make him dual text books about his own family, and this was used for focused work on literacy at home and at school. Where children, like Abdullah for instance, are causing concern at school, we need to examine whether the teaching strategies used are taking account of the child's linguistic and cultural experiences and concerns. We need to work with parents to create appropriate learning materials and opportunities for their children, in and out of school. Many schools have successfully used strategies like inviting parents in to write with their children in the home language through family writing workshops, or as part of the work of the classroom. The way these materials are then used is crucial to the status of the children and parents, their languages and cultures.

Developing strategies that address inequality

It is impossible to talk about issues of language and culture without taking note of the power relationships that they embody. In schools, parents are less powerful than teachers at the best of times. In trying to work with bilingual parents, who are often the least powerful members of our society, thought has to be given as to how to approach parents to address their real concerns, how to give them a real voice, how to tap into their experience and knowledge in a way that will benefit them, their children and the school.

Some schools have addressed this through having meetings for particular groups of parents. This has worked best where a community group or representative has been involved. For instance in one school, a Bengali community group acted as an intermediary between the school and the Bengali speaking parents who were invited in to discuss their children's low levels of achievement and problems in the school. The community group chaired the meeting and put the parents and school in more equal positions. This led to the Bengali parents setting up a Bengali literacy Saturday class in the school, with the help of school staff. The Bengali parents, particularly the mothers, are a very vocal group and committed in their support of school initiatives, and the children's self esteem and achievement has risen. In another school, a West African member of staff set up a parents discussion group for West African parents where they were able to set the agenda, invite speakers, and take control of their learning about English schooling.

In order to help children achieve their best, teachers need time to reflect on children's talk and writing, time to talk to parents in depth, and time to develop strategies that will meet these diverse needs and include parents as genuine partners. We all know that time is in short supply, but where there is a whole-school commitment, these things can and do happen.

References

Bettelheim, B. (1978) *The Uses of Enchantment*. London: Penguin.
Brice Heath, S. (1983) *Ways with Words*. Cambridge: Cambridge University Press.
Burgess, T. and Hardcastle, J. (1991) 'A Tale of Three Learners: the cultural dimension of classroom language learning', in Gordon, P. *Teaching the Humanities*. Essex: Woburn Press.
Gregory, E. (1994) 'Cultural Assumptions and Early Years Pedagogy: the effect of the home culture on minority children's interpretation of reading in school', *Language Culture and Curriculum*, 7, 2.
Hall, S. (1992) 'The Question of Cultural Identity', in Hall, S., Held and McGrew *Modernity and its Future*. Cambridge: Polity Press.
ILEA (1983) *Stories in the Multilingual Classroom*. London: ILEA Learning Resources Branch.
Savitsky, F. (1994) *Bilingual Children: a guide for parents*. Southwark: Language and Literacy Unit.
Tizard, B., Blatchford, P., Burke, J., Farquar, C. and Plewis, I. (1988) *Young Children at School in the Inner City*. London: Laurence Erlbaum Associates.

5 Minimising obstacles, maximising opportunities: teachers and black parents

Beverley Crooks

Introduction

It would seem safe to assume from the presence of black people in Britain for centuries and in much larger numbers since the 1950s, that black parents are as informed about their children's education as white parents, are fully involved in school activities and regularly help in schools. In fact the opposite is true: research spanning the last thirty years has consistently drawn attention to the significant absence of black[1] parents in schools. The experiences of black pupils in the British education system have not been successful for many. These have also been well documented and undoubtedly influence the relationships parents have with schools. It would therefore be simplistic to discuss positive parental involvement strategies for black parents without acknowledging the constraints and obstacles they face.

The absence of black parents from school-based activities has concerned home–school liaison teachers for some time. The central focus of this chapter is to look at some of the reasons for this with specific reference to black parents' and pupils' experience of school, their achievement and the disproportionately high exclusion rate of black children from school. It concludes by offering some tried and tested strategies for involving black parents in school.

Black parents' experience of school

Research has shown that all parents have much in common in wanting their children to succeed academically, wanting to understand what their children actually do at school and wanting to support their learning. However, no two parents or children are the same, nor will they have the same needs. Race, class, gender, education and socio-economic status all heterogenise parents, and just as Asian, white and black parents often have different expectations and different experiences of the education system, so teachers have different views of parents from each group. It is timely to focus on the issues of black parents as recent changes in Home Office funding to support ethnic minority pupils have prioritised bilingual learners and their parents, so marginalising African-Caribbean learners and their parents since most speak English as a first language. This emphasis on bilingual needs would give no cause for concern if black children were not underachieving or being excluded to the extent that they currently are, but the general pattern to emerge from studies of the educational performance of different ethnic groups is that black children are still obtaining significantly lower scores than white children (Swann 1985, Drew and Gray 1990, OFSTED 1996).

The current attention to barriers between parents and teachers arising from linguistic and cultural differences ignores the possible impact racism might have upon the educational experience of many teachers and parents. The impression given is that in order to counteract educational underachievement and improve relations between teachers and black parents, it is necessary to fund initiatives which compensate for the linguistic and cultural deficiencies of ethnic minority communities. The focus of concern then becomes not on the structure of society or the system of schooling but on the individual and family pathology of ethnic minority groups. The danger of such a focus, especially as 98 per cent of teachers are white, is that it could reinforce a process in which teachers perceive underachievement as related to the family background and cultures of black pupils (Bagley 1992). However, the literature in the 1990s suggests that educational professionals still regard black parents as posing problems for schools, instead of focusing attention on the school.

Black parents who are deeply committed to their children's education, however, are not always sufficiently confident or feel welcomed by teachers to come into the school. Many of them are intimidated by the hostile environment of schools and are reluctant to enter classrooms to discuss issues relating to their own children, let alone help in the school generally. The following sections offer some reasons why.

It is unfortunate but none the less the case that there exists in our society an unwritten code of conduct that allows institutions and their staff to exercise authority over patrons. In this way, doctors exercise authority over patients: as it is assumed that the doctor knows about medicine and the patient does not, it is likewise assumed that the teacher knows about education and the parent does not. So as it seems right and proper for the doctor to control the course of consultation and treatment of a compliant patient, so are teachers as professionals in the position to control the content and delivery of what is taught, with parents apparently having only to comply and co-operate. If such experiences are common to most parents, what of the experience of black parents? In establishing a positive basis for black parents to enter the classroom, teachers must take the lead: they are the ones with the power.

Whereas it would be true to say that in the 1960s and 1970s many black parents in Britain had the disadvantage of not having experienced the education system their children were passing through, by the 1990s many of the parents having difficulty overcoming barriers to working with schools have themselves been educated in Britain and are all too familiar with the systen here. What could be the explanation for the negative experience of black parents in the present education system and the persistent absence of black parents from the classroom? For the answer to these questions we have to look at the experience of black children in education.

Black children's experience of school

The Office for Standards in Education (OFSTED 1996) published a report highlighting disturbing evidence that black boys are entering school at age five with academic performance levels equal to those of their peers, and yet by the age of seven are underachieving in maths and science. What is happening in the first two years of education to bring this about? Those advocating a colour-blind approach in schools are failing to recognise the reality that staff, like other people, do treat people differently on the basis of perceived 'racial' characteristics.

There have been a number of studies that assess the experience of black pupils in British schools, starting with Coard (1971) and more recently in Channer (1995). These studies conclude that black pupils experience a disproportionate amount of conflict and criticism from white teachers. For example, it is not unusual for teachers to discuss a child's family background at length, usually in the staff room over coffee, often making assumptions and judgements based on little or no evidence. Tizard *et al.* (1988) conducted research in this area and asked white teachers about their experience of black parents: 70 per cent mentioned a negative attribute in their reply. Many of the views held by teachers about parents seem to be uninformed, judgemental and incorrect. Wright (1992) stated from her research that it was apparent from teachers' comments that their perceptions of the catchment area served by the school had a particular effect on what they were trying to achieve in the school. Many teachers perceived the catchment area and the black children's backgrounds as adversely affecting the school. There were constant references to perceived problems related to family structure. However, it is not uncommon for teachers to admit that they need to know more about the communities they work with. Clark (1983) argues that too often teachers discuss family composition (that is, single parent, child living with grandmother and others), and not family disposition such as beliefs and values. Many teachers hold the view that much of society's ills can be attributed to children who do not have the advantage of a stable two-parent family. Crooks (1993) provides the following example of a student, Kamau, who wanted to set the record straight in light of his own experience:

> In terms of family background, I felt fortunate to come from a two income family – my mother brought me up alone and had two jobs, hence two incomes to

support me! I never felt deprived or in need. My extended family, my grandparents in particular, played an essential role in providing stability, positive cultural environment and positive male role models for me.

Teachers hold opinions about different groups of parents and the degree to which they support education and this has implications for the expectations teachers have of black children.

Not all parents have had a positive experience of education themselves, and because most draw on past experiences to make judgements about the present, some parents may be led to negative views about teachers and schools; feelings of disempowerment together with lack of confidence may also contribute to the distance between teachers and black parents. Many black parents opt to support learning outside the classroom; supplementary schools, personal tutors and encyclopedias are well established features of black communities around the country. Supplementary schools with their emphasis on high educational standards continue to thrive as they provide pupils and parents with a sense of academic achievement and a feeling of being 'understood' by teachers. One aspect of supplementary schools that black parents often comment on relates to parents and teachers communicating openly and honestly about children's academic achievement in a secure, open and informal environment. It is important to note that most supplementary schools operating in the black community are staffed by black teachers and volunteers.

These schools not only aim to raise pupils' achievement but also to improve self-esteem by providing positive role models in the form of teachers and a curriculum providing an insight into culture and history that fosters a sense of pride among pupils. Teachers from these schools often comment to parents that they see no evidence of the unruly behaviour reported from mainstream teachers. This implies that some significance can be attached to the teaching and learning styles experienced by pupils in the two different settings (Callender 1995). Parents generally support the level of work expected from teachers in supplementary schools and at home and become frustrated to find out that pupils do not always transfer these high standards into the classroom. Why is this? Teachers in supplementary schools value and show respect for parents, are prepared to invest time and are genuinely interested in each parent as an individual. This sort of interest and respect helps create a solid basis for some parents to develop a positive relationship with the teacher and furthermore feel confident enough to volunteer to help in supplementary schools. Many black parents are more likely to be parent governors, help with fundraising, assist with school outings and offer a particular skill required by the school to enhance the curriculum offered. A recent review of parental involvement initiatives (Holden *et al.* 1996) reveals that very few black parents work in the classroom on a regular basis. However, for parents to participate in the classroom there must be a real and obvious commitment from teachers.

Current concerns

Research carried out by Wright (1992) revealed that black boys were considered by teachers to exhibit disruptive behaviour in class. Consequently black boys feature more frequently among the most reprimanded and controlled group in the classroom. Further it was observed that black boys were likely to be singled out for reprimanding even where several children from other ethnic groups were engaged in the same behaviour. It was not surprising therefore to find that black boys were over-represented in the school's disciplinary system. In the study, teachers held stereotypes of black boys which tended to be totally negative, thus providing the basis for negative expectations that influenced their judgements of children's ability. In an attempt to sort out such 'problems' schools tend to initiate contact with parents; previously informal communication becomes formalised when there is a problem or crisis. The only contact that some black parents have with school is on these terms, hardly an ideal basis on which to build a relationship. The Children Act (1989) and the Special Education Needs Code of Practice (1993) both require greater involvement of parents throughout any process developed by the school to meet children's individual needs; yet some black parents increasingly find themselves attending the school principally to sort out 'problems' and at times of crisis. The last national figures on exclusion from school to be analysed by ethnic origin relate to the early 1990s.These suggest that African-Caribbean students are four times more likely to be excluded from school than their white peers (Gillborn 1996). Let us not forget that the negative experiences of black children are also shared by black parents.

While black parents are no different from white parents in wanting to support their children's education and receive more information about their child's daily routine and curriculum, it is interesting to note that on the whole it is white parents who cross the threshold and help in the classroom; it is less common for black parents to help in the classroom on a regular basis. Research carried out by Holden, Hughes and Desforges (1996) concluded that there is a general feeling among parents that they should not be the first to offer to come into the classroom, but that the teacher should instigate this if she/he felt it necessary:

'If the teacher wants me to help I will do it.'
'She just needs to ask me.'

Parents in the study recognised that helping in the classroom was one way of becoming more informed and provided an opportunity for them to find out how they could support their children's learning. They wanted to help but were waiting to be invited by the teacher. One can safely conclude from this example that if black parents are not being asked to assist in the classroom, they may well be less informed about the curriculum and have fewer strategies at their disposal to support their children's learning. It is worth mentioning at this point that some parents prefer not to become involved in schools or help in the classroom, preferring to leave the domain for the professionals and respecting the territory of the teacher.

To increase the numbers of black parents in the classroom, teachers have much to do and much to learn. There is a clear need for further research to be carried out focusing on the strengths of black families and the contribution they can make to children's learning inside and outside school. It is unfortunate that the valuable resource that black parents can provide to schools is seldom recognised, especially by teachers.

In the remainder of the chapter attention is turned to positive and forward looking strategies for teachers committed to promoting the active involvement of black parents in the classroom.

CASE STUDY

The following case study provides a useful working example based on real practice observed in one inner-city primary school with 280 pupils, of which 35 per cent are black.

The appointment of a new headteacher heralded the end of a long tradition of black and Asian parents not helping in the classroom and the beginning of a number of new initiatives to increase parental involvement generally in the school with specific attention paid to those parents distanced from the learning process for a variety of reasons. The school instigated the initiatives and utilised support from the LEA to develop the work. The headteacher identified herself as a crucial agent for change in the school and played an important role in assisting teachers and parents to identify what the school could do to increase parental involvement. The headteacher took full responsibility for establishing and maintaining systems to monitor and support the initiatives.

The role of the local education authority

Although local education authorities no longer have the resources to support schools in the way they once did, prior to budget delegation to schools the primary school in question was located in an LEA that still recognises the need to support schools delivering high educational standards.

The annual headteachers conference focused on the issue of parental involvement in schools. Black parents were invited to the conference and workshops and speakers provided an important framework for the discussions that took place. Topics included cross-cultural communication strategies, dealing with conflict, African-Caribbean parenting techniques, expectations, perceptions and experiences. Funding was secured from central government to employ an advisor to assist local schools to develop effective strategies for involving parents in children's learning. The service was offered to schools at no additional cost. The Information Centre, initially set up to meet the factual needs of employees, extended its services to meet the growing demand from parents who welcomed the opportunity to receive information from an impartial source.

Local inspectors identified parental involvement strategies as a special focus during visits to all schools in the local authority. Link inspectors for each school devised a series of key issues for schools to consider to assist them monitor and evaluate their strategies for involving parents. The job descriptions of teachers working in the Language Development Service clearly state their responsibilities to develop closer links between teachers and parents who have English as an additional language. Teachers' performance was carefully monitored and assessed at the end of each term.

Special Educational Needs Co-ordinators throughout the local authority were provided with specially designed courses delivered at the teachers centre and school. The aim of the courses was to provide teachers with the opportunity to explore strategies to assist them in involving parents in the process of assessment, to help meet individual learning needs and help parents to identify appropriate ways of supporting children through individual learning programmes. Training was specifically designed for parent governors, since on the whole governor training does not always appreciate the unique relationship that parents as governors have with the school and the parent body as a whole. Furthermore, the LEA recognised they needed support in order to present the views often expressed by parents in the playground and in the local community. The training assisted in a proactive way that helped to reinforce the status of black governors, aiming to provide the support and advice governors themselves identified as necessary to carry out the role effectively and with confidence. A support group was established for and by black governors in the local authority.

Finally, the equal opportunities policy recognised that the education system currently provides unequal opportunities for black pupils and parents, resulting in unequal outcomes. The LEA also acknowledged its role and responsibility in identifying barriers which impede the progress of pupils and parents. The LEA fully endorsed any school's attempts to achieve the above through a change both in understanding and action.

Subsequent action

The support structure described above enabled the school to develop the following initiatives. The advisory teacher was responsible for assisting the school to recognise the need for a whole-school approach to developing effective strategies for supporting both teachers and parents in their attempts to involve parents in children's learning and raise levels of achievement. The school was encouraged to articulate the vision it had for the teachers and parents, identifying exactly what it wanted to achieve. This vision had to be clearly stated and agreed by all teachers so that they were all aware of what they were working towards and furthermore would recognise it when they had achieved it. Although concerned to develop tangibly by introducing a parents' room, parents' notice board, newsletter and classes to meet parents' own learning and information needs, the school was even more concerned with the need to change the negative perceptions some parents had of the school and some teachers had of parents. The school decided to develop its policy from the good practice it was about to implement.

A set of guidelines and procedures for teachers was developed at the same time to ensure consistent practice throughout all key stages. The policy was an ongoing document that was shaped and adapted to reflect current good practice. Instead of using the LEA's agency for the recruitment and selection of staff the headteacher broke with tradition and designed her own advertisements for publications other than the Guardian and Times Educational Supplement. The adverts clearly stated the ethnic origin of the pupils on roll at the school, together with an appeal for black staff (covered by the Race Relations Act 1976, Section 5(2)(d) allowing employers to specify the ethnic origin of potential employees). As a result the school employed its first black teacher.

A member of staff was appointed as home–school links co-ordinator. In order to fulfil the aims set out in the school development plan, the Co-ordinator developed a job description in consultation with colleagues and parents. Long- and short-term targets were set; additionally targets were set to be achieved by the end of each term throughout the next academic year. The school development plan clearly stated the school's intentions over a three year period to work with parents. Human and financial resources were identified and allocated. The governing body was informed of the school's intentions to develop concrete ways of involving black parents. Governors supported the initiative, demonstrating their support and commitment by undertaking to ensure that as vacancies occurred they would take steps to fill them with a black person. Parents were involved from the initial phases to develop the action plans. The school continued to use the advisor to research the nature of the interactions between teachers and parents. Findings from the research provided useful information for the teachers and highlighted specific areas for teachers to focus on during their in-service training and their interaction with parents.

Proposals for black parents

Individual schools should have their own priorities in setting up strategies for working with a particular groups of parents. Below are some initiatives undertaken by the school in question:

- The school developed its purpose, aims, ethos, behaviour management and approach to teaching and learning in consultation with black parents, providing teachers with valuable professional development and the opportunity to test and refute stereotypes.

- An induction programme for newly qualified teachers provided support and guidance on communicating with parents together with opportunities for the development of interpersonal skills. Teachers and parents were encouraged to avoid allowing preconceived ideas and prejudices to influence interaction with black pupils and parents.
- Teachers committed extra time and effort before, after and during school to make initial contacts with parents, listen to parents' concerns, take action and generally to put policy into practice.
- Close scrutiny of the behaviour management policy led to an honest appraisal of its implementation, with specific reference to black children.
- Individual support teachers working in the school targeted pupils at risk of being excluded from school early. Home–school teacher, parents and class teacher liaised to reduce the likelihood of exclusion.
- The advisor monitored the existing means of parental involvement to improve liaison and was available as mediator if invited by teachers or parents, leading to an enlightened approach and improved relationships.
- Systems were set in place to monitor the academic performance of black children. At the beginning of the year, the school tested reading ability and set a target to improve reading levels.
- An after-school homework club was established with the help of teachers and supplementary school, to provide additional learning opportunities outside school.
- School curricula were reviewed and adapted to accommodate the different religious and cultural backgrounds of pupils.
- A safe environment was provided for parents to raise issues without fear of retribution or adverse affect on their children. Parents acted as evaluators, parents were asked for feedback to assess how the school was meeting the needs of black parents and children.

Four years later

The impact of activities carried out by the school in targeting black parents and pupils resulted in the following changes four years after implementation:

- A significant improvement in the academic performance of black pupils in reading. Contributions to this development included improved teaching strategies and the implementation of individual learning programmes designed by class teachers to be completed in homework club and at home with parents. Until the school began to monitor, they were unaware of the extent to which black children were underachieving.
- More black parents were visible in school during the day, in the classrooms and supporting the school generally. This was due partly to par-

ents of reception age children being adopted by parents of Year 1 children and so on through all the key stages, providing parents with an opportunity to share information, views and experiences informally with each other.

- Black staff were represented at different levels of the school's hierarchy, including senior management and governors. Previously, black staff worked as cleaners and in the kitchen. This development had a positive influence on all parents and in particular on the status of black parents and pupils.

- A parent volunteer course was developed for all parents interested in helping in classrooms. Fifteen parents completed the course, resulting in two parents progressing to higher education courses. Parents are now more actively involved in children's learning in school. Five black parents regularly help in classrooms; two parents help in the homework club after school.

- A review of the behaviour management policy, with specific reference to race, resulted in a positive and supportive environment in classrooms and fewer fixed-term and permanent exclusions of black pupils.

- Parents' knowledge and understanding of the curriculum were improved by day and evening workshops. Information was recorded and distributed to inform parents unable to attend workshops.

- A parents' file was created and translated copies made available. A large folder was designed and issued to each parent. The parents' file provided general information, at the appropriate time, on loose sheets, such as curricular aims and objectives, assessment, monitoring and progress, specific ways parents could support children's learning at home and key issues relating to the school's approach to teaching, reading and maths.

- A course was designed for parents interested in volunteering time to the school, providing an opportunity for parents and teachers to learn about each other in a training environment. Both parents' and teachers' views of each other improved significantly.

- The school worked with teachers from a local supplementary school to design and teach a history project.

- Teachers admitted to having fewer negative perceptions of black parents and pupils and a better understanding of the families and communities they serve, and began to value and respect the contribution parents made to learning. Parents' views of teachers also improved. The advisor was used less and less to mediate between teachers and parents as relationships improved.

The case study above suggests there are many ways in which teachers can involve black parents in the classroom and that a range of methods and strategies is required if all parents are to be reached.

Last word

Relationships between parents and teachers do not exist in a vacuum: the context in which they meet plays a crucial role in shaping their perspectives and expectations. Any development within a school must recognise the need to take the lead and be proactive by identifying a developmental, supportive and positive approach to involving black parents. To shape and influence development and change, teachers need to improve standards of teaching; create opportunities for parents to raise issues of concern and for teachers to listen to and respond effectively and efficiently to the concerns parents may have; involve parents in the heart of the issue and not leave them stranded on the periphery; and avoid a tokenistic approach to cultural diversity and parental involvement. While some teachers maintain they are unable to invest the time and effort necessary to improve the overall experience of black pupils and parents in school, others have come to realise that they can no longer afford not to.

Notes

1. The term black will be used to describe African Caribbean parents and pupils, including those British born of African and Caribbean origin.

References

Bagley, C. (1992) *Back to the Future – Section 11 of the local Government Act 1966: LEAs and multicultural/antiracist education*. Windsor: NFER.

Callender, C. (1995) 'A Question of Style: black teachers and pupils in multi ethnic schools', in *Language and Education*, 9, 3, pp.145–59.

Channer, Y. (1995) *I am a Promise – the school achievement of British African Caribbeans*. Stoke-on-Trent: Trentham Books.

Clark, R.M. (1983) *Family Life and School Achievement: why poor black children succeed or fail*. Chicago: University of Chicago Press.

Coard, B. (1971) *How the West Indian Child is Made Educationally Subnormal in the British School System*. London: New Beacon Books.

Crooks, B. (1993) *Language and Identity – an investigation into the language repertoire of black pupils and parents*. Unpublished MA thesis. London: Thames Valley University.

Duncan, C. (1989) 'Home, School and Community in a Multiracial Context', in Wolfendale, S. (Ed.) *Parental Involvement: Developing Networks between School, Home and Community*. London: Cassell.

Drew, D. and Gray, J. (1990) 'The Black White Gap in Exam Achievement: a statistical critique of a decade's research'. Paper presented at the British Sociological Association annual conference, University of Surrey.

Gillborn, D. (1996) *Exclusions from School: Croydon in Context*. London: Institute of Education, University of London.

Holden, C., Hughes, M. and Desforges, C. (1996) 'Equally informed? Ethnic minority parents, schools and assessment', in. *Multicultural Teaching Volume*, 14, 3, pp.16–20.

Mirza, H.S. (1992) *Young, Female and Black*. London: Routledge.

OFSTED (1996) *Recent Research on the Achievement of Ethnic Minority Pupils*. London: HMSO.

Swann, M. (1985) *Education for All. Final Report of the Committee of Inquiry into the Education of Children from Ethnic Minority Groups*. London: HMSO.

Tizard, B., Mortimore, J. and Burchell, B. (1988) 'Involving Parents from Minority Groups', in Bastiani, J. (Ed.) *Parents and Teachers 2: From Policy to Practice*. Windsor: NFER-Nelson.

Wright, C. (1992) *Race Relations in the Primary School*. London: David Fulton.

6 Home–school work with Traveller children and their families

Margaret Wood

Introduction

Many people have never stopped to consider how Traveller children fit into the formal education system. Despite LEAs' duty to make appropriate provision for all school age children in their area and parents' responsibility to ensure that their children receive efficient full-time education, significant numbers of Traveller children are not gaining full access. The reasons for this are many. At the present time, maybe a third of children of statutory school age are not registered. The majority of these non-enrolments are at secondary level. It has been estimated (DfEE 1996) that 80 to 85 per cent of eleven to fourteen year olds and 95 per cent of fourteen to sixteen year olds are out of school. Even when children are on a school roll, attendance is often erratic, with fifteen weeks out of forty weeks present being the average. As children get older, they often attend less frequently until they drop out altogether. The almost inevitable consequence for children whose attendance is intermittent is a lack of continuity leading to underachievement and a corresponding sense of failure and demotivation. Improved enrolment depends almost entirely upon the co-operation of parents and, as with all children, regular attendance and the fulfilment of potential are likely outcomes if families and schools are working in partnership.

The Swann Report (DES 1985), the HMI discussion paper 'The Education of Travellers' Children' (DES 1983) and two European resolutions (Council of Europe 1989) all highlight the particular educational needs of children from Traveller communities. Many LEAs receive grant funding under Section 488 of the 1996 Education Act for projects to address these needs. The guidance on good practice (DES Circular 10/90) underlines the crucial importance of close liaison with Traveller parents:

> It is common experience that links with Travellers, as with all parents, need to be built on trusting relationships. This is important if accurate information is to be gathered on the range and level of educational needs, and to ensure Travellers' full participation in the education system.

For the past eight years I have worked as a peripatetic teacher in the

Cambridgeshire County Team for Traveller Education. My accountabilities include 'home visits to encourage parental involvement in schools' and 'visiting the sites of fairs and circuses to promote and develop distance learning'. The majority of my teaching is in two village colleges and I have an outreach and liaison role with families and primary schools in their catchment areas. I also support city primary schools where Traveller parents have traditionally refused to allow their children to transfer from Year 6 to Year 7.

Before discussing in more detail the significant issues for Traveller families, it may be helpful to provide some background information. The term 'Traveller' can be misleading. Travellers are not members of a homogeneous community, although those who describe themselves as Travellers may have things in common. In Cambridgeshire there are Travellers of Gypsy background, there are Irish, Scottish, Welsh and English Travellers, there are Showpeople and Circus families as well as small numbers of New Travellers. Some Travellers live in houses, others live in trailers or mobile homes on private, public or unauthorised sites. Families may be highly nomadic, others travel seasonally, and some never move.

There are examples of Traveller parents successfully supporting their children's schooling and some of these will be described later. There are Travellers who serve as school governors as well as some teachers and other professionals of Traveller background. However, many schools identify a general lack of involvement of Traveller parents as a cause for concern. They recognise that cultural differences as well as fragmented schooling are significant, but they are unsure how to respond.

The family perspective

A better understanding of the current situation may be gained by examining how it came about. Traveller parents of today were themselves of school age twenty to thirty years ago. Many of them did not attend school and among those who did, many had negative experiences and feel that the time spent there was of little benefit. The Plowden Report (DES 1967) noted that up to nine out of ten Traveller children were not attending school. The Schools Council report (Reiss 1975) estimated 10 to 25 per cent attendance in 1969–70. The Swann Report (DES 1985), which devoted a whole chapter to the educational needs of Traveller children, confirmed this picture, explaining that 'this widespread non-attendance at school is unique to Travellers' children and lies at the heart of their plight'. Nowadays, Traveller children, especially at primary level, are gaining better access to their educational entitlement, but there is still a considerable way to go.

Parents recall that constant moves and difficulties in finding a place to stop, coupled with hostility and lack of understanding on the part of many schools meant that what little time they spent in classrooms was of little value. Even those who attended more regularly speak of the irrelevance of what they were taught and a sense of frustration that they left school barely literate. Their overriding memories are of isolation and failure. Teachers' low expectations of them were apparently confirmed. What chance did they have when they were told to colour in pictures at the back of the room and when more settled children were advised by their parents to keep well away from them? Even when Travellers did succeed in obtaining a qualification, certain employers would ignore their job applications as soon as they discovered their origins.

In this context, it is hardly surprising that some parents are extremely wary of the effect schools might have on their children. School represents a culture and values with which they feel they cannot identify and to which, in some respects, they do not wish to subscribe. Travellers traditionally live in close-knit communities where children are supported by an extended family of grandparents, aunts, uncles and cousins. Sites tend to be geographically isolated, either outside or on the fringes of towns and villages. Members of the local housed populations regularly show an alarming depth of prejudice and antagonism, particularly towards families who live on large sites or in unauthorised places, unaware that, with the acute national shortage of licensed sites, the provisions of the 1994 Criminal Justice and Public Order Act and the constraints of planning law, many Travellers have little choice but to stop illegally. In some ways, the situation has not changed since the sixteenth century, when merely to be a Gypsy was a capital offence.

A family's travelling pattern is by no means the only factor affecting their children's attendance, continuity of schooling and educational achievement. As I have already indicated, not all Travellers travel. Part of the difficulty derives from the mismatch between the parents' attitudes and expectations and those of teachers and schools. In Britain, Travellers belong to a relatively small minority ethnic group. Despite economic interdependence, they have traditionally lived at a remove from the majority society, which tends to expect them to 'conform', ignoring their cultural and linguistic distinctiveness. Similar attitudes are mirrored in schools, which may interpret Travellers' behaviour as wantonly deviant. A parent recently explained that the school was mistaken in judging her son's behaviour as intentionally anti-social. His actions stemmed from his confusion about the two very different worlds in which he is expected to operate. At home, he is free to run around outside, to repair motors with the men and to breed rare chickens. At school, he is seen as a small child and expected to observe a set of incomprehensible rules, such as lining up in silence, keeping off the grass and mixing with his own age group. Other misunderstandings arise in connection with pupils' traditional gold jewellery, their unwillingness to change for PE and failure to complete home–work. Closer home–school links can go a long way to resolving conflicts, by enabling parents and teachers to understand the constraints each has to face and to accommodate one another's values.

No two Traveller families hold identical views on their children's educational needs, but discussions with many different families reveal a number of common threads. Teachers who seriously wish to involve them more fully in the life of the school need to be sensitive to their perspective. Anxious to preserve their own culture, many express a very real fear that their children may be persuaded to give up their identity and reject the teachings of the home. They worry about bad influences, including sex, drugs and other children who, in their opinion, may have been brought up too liberally. Sometimes other families actively encourage rejection of school. Some parents will not risk embarrassing older children who have missed out on early years schooling or have had too many gaps. Almost invariably, parents of younger children want them to attend school because they believe that skills learnt there will be useful to them, but once a child can read and write, they consider it is time to leave school. Some parents believe that school should be optional or part time and that they should not insist if their child refuses to attend.

A serious concern is that children may suffer bullying and racial harassment and that, in a situation where the various family members are separated into different classes, there will be no support at moments of crisis. Although many schools now have strong anti-racist and equal opportunities policies, parents hear what is being said by members of local communities, in the press and by councils: 'Travellers are not welcome'. In the end, some parents are so fearful that they opt for 'Education Otherwise',[1] they move away or they send their child to stay with a relative. School, as far as they are concerned, is about schooling in the '3R's' . It is the parents' role to educate their children for adult life.

The school perspective

In their discussion of home–school relations with parents from minority groups, Tizard, Mortimore and Burchell (1988) recognise the potential difficulties for teachers of explaining their aims and methods to parents from different cultures and the undesirability in certain circumstances of complying with parents' demands, but they go on to say that 'unless schools are prepared to discuss [such] points of view, and go some way towards meeting them, they cannot hope to enlist parental support for their work'. In their dealings with Traveller parents, it is particularly important for schools to listen hard and to show a willingness to take the first step.

Teachers' attitudes and expectations influence pupils' classroom performance. Few teachers have had opportunities to acquire unbiased knowledge of Travellers, or they consider it unnecessary to do so, and some mistakenly believe that by 'treating everyone the same' and ignoring children's home culture and circumstances they are offering equal opportunities to all. This clearly favours those children who share the background of their teachers. The portrayal of Travellers in literature and the media, the main source of information for most non-Travellers, is frequently stereotyped, oscillating from the exotic image of the 'true Romany', 'free spirit' on the one hand to the feckless criminal and outcast on the other. Lack of direct contact with Travellers means that teachers know little of their social structures, their language, their culture and beliefs. Some find it hard to accept that parents who really care deeply about their children's right to education and future happiness do not consider school a priority. They are indignant and uncomprehending that a whole range of other matters can take precedence, from sorting out drainage problems on the site, to buying clothes for a family wedding, attending a Christian convention or choosing a new horse. Nor may schools judge a child by the same yardstick as the parents. A child deemed to have special needs at school may be respected as the scholar of the family.

Linking home and school

Jean-Pierre Liégois (Liégois 1994) stresses the importance of 'convergence' which 'implies consultation, and consultation [which] in turn implies a two-way dialogue'. He goes on to identify an often missing aspect of home–school relations:

> while efforts are sometimes made to explain the school to Traveller parents, it is rare indeed for equivalent effort to be made to explain the Traveller context (history, culture, etc…) to the school and those who work in it.
>
> (Liégois 1994)

Schools often speak of home–school links when effectively they mean the opposite.

Parental or family involvement is generally recognised as a key feature of school effectiveness but it can operate at a number of levels. There is the statutory requirement to report to parents and carers on children's progress, but most schools go further than this. At the simplest level, they send home information about parents' evenings and fundraising events, but there is increasing recognition of the value of encouraging parents to contribute to the curriculum by sharing their skills within the school. What opportunities for this are created for Traveller parents? Through parent governors, in particular, parents have the chance to participate in decision making. What positive moves do schools make to recruit Traveller governors? Are Traveller parents encouraged to join in the consultation process during OFSTED inspections? In none of these areas has sufficient progress yet been made.

An issue that needs to be considered is whether it is appropriate to make special arrangements to promote the involvement of Traveller families. It could be argued that all parents are equally free to avail themselves of opportunities to participate in parents' evenings, the PTA, and parent-governor selection. However, on reflection, it is clear that the same factors that tend to exclude the children from the system also alienate some parents. The 'open door' policy does not work. The philosophy behind the Section 488 grant acknowledges the place of positive discrimination, at least as a temporary measure, and particular arrangements which take account of individual needs, whether initiated by the Traveller team or by the school are simply a means to ensuring that unnecessary obstacles to participation are removed. On occasions, it may be beneficial for schools to issue individual invitations to Traveller parents or even to organise specific events, for example to discuss areas of common concern such as sex education or how parents can maintain their children's progress during unavoidable absences from school.

Enrolment

Some Traveller parents register their children at school or nursery as a matter of course, believing that they deserve the chances they never had. Others hold back, either because of their convictions or because the family has more urgent preoccupations. If, for example, the council is taking action to evict them, if they do not have ready access to water and toilet facilities, if the work is elsewhere or if there has been a family crisis such as bad health or a bereavement, school is unlikely to come first. A home–school liaison officer, whose main responsibility is outreach to children not on a school roll, may have to make a series of visits, anticipating the questions families wish to ask and showing patience and understanding in the face of resistance. It may be useful to bring a teacher to meet the family and arrange a preliminary visit to the school, as parents need to be reassured that their children will be safe and happy in that new and unfamiliar environment. At the secondary transfer stage, once again the family's confidence may need to be developed, for example, by attending open evenings with them, by arranging individual visits to the secondary school or by inviting a small group of primary parents to talk informally with a few teachers and pupils, including Travellers, from both schools. As with so many things, fear of the unknown is far worse than the reality.

Home visits

Much of the home–school work of Traveller education teams is designed to pave the way for improved dialogue between the various parties involved. In many instances, Section 210 teachers and home–school liaison officers act as intermediaries, attempting to develop trusting relationships and to raise awareness in the hope that, eventually, direct lines of communication will be established. With both groups, what is often required is to stimulate greater self-reliance and flexibility. Home visits, often involving a Traveller team member, are sometimes the most effective way of smoothing over difficulties in school, as letters run the risk of being misread or misinterpreted. A telephone call is sometimes appropriate, but a face-to-face discussion can be invaluable if, for instance, a child's attendance is erratic, either for providing an explanation or for persuading parents of the benefits of continuity. Many parents welcome the opportunity to talk over school matters in the security of their own home, though others are pleased if the class teacher takes the initiative to get to know them at the school gate. Schools which include home visiting to all families as part of their normal induction programme sometimes arrange for class teachers to visit the home of new Traveller pupils mid-year and this can make parents feel more at ease when they later meet in school. Parents are always interested in photographs of their children and dropping one in at home can be a good excuse for a visit, and a means of getting to know the family and using this knowledge as a point of reference in the classroom.

Over the threshold

One obvious method of encouraging parents to come into school is to make sure that they receive an overt welcome from the head and staff on their first visit. In the early days, an effective way of supporting parents with consultation meetings has been for a team member to make a home visit beforehand to explain the purpose of the meeting and to offer to accompany them. Some secondary schools make the situation less awesome by suggesting that parents attend with their child, or by arranging an interview with just one teacher. When children are fully included from the outset in whatever is going on in school, if they are given parts in plays and assemblies, if their work is on show and displays and resources reflect Travellers and their culture alongside other cultures, then parents, including fathers, will be motivated to come in and have a look.

Parents and families who are asked for contributions they feel capable of giving will come forward, bringing their culture with them and making the school a richer place for all children. One school that has always welcomed Travellers was presented by the children's grandparents with an arrangement of traditional paper flowers in a handmade wicker basket, a wonderful resource for the whole school. An aunt brought in her chrome cans, buckets and bowls to talk to a class that was doing a topic on water. Another parent invited her daughter's class, who were studying homes, to visit her chalet and trailer. One mother was interviewed by a Year 10 class that was studying minorities. Families who collect scrap have offered items for classroom museums and a father who deals in carpets has donated off-cuts for the reading corner. A mother who does not read or write is helping in a junior class with sewing. Some parents who were worried about their children's swimming classes and class outings have been invited to join in, and lunchtime behaviour difficulties have been alleviated through bringing in mothers as additional supervisors. Various parents have been willing to explain to groups of teachers about their children's educational needs. By recognising and valuing parents' many skills, schools are likely to develop their commitment to the children's formal education, thereby improving attendance and achievement. When Traveller parents routinely take part in activities alongside non-Traveller parents and teachers, people begin to see one another as human beings and negative attitudes start to disappear.

Examples of initiatives

Parents are naturally proud when their children's achievements are acknowledged, particularly in tangible form. One project organised by the county team produced 'Common Ground', an anthology of children's writing, including some Anglo-Romani, illustrated with photographs and drawings by the children, and distributed to families. Even less confident readers, have shown an enormous interest in the book, particularly when they have recognised their own or their friends' children. We have been encouraged to plan further small publications, adapting the detail according to the demands of particular areas and schools.

Inter-agency co-operation is very important when working with Traveller families, and team members have supported a Community Education initiative based in a village college near Ely. Secondary Traveller pupils attended twilight sessions to prepare materials for a new anthology, 'Paper Flowers'. Their parents and friends were invited to contribute and many lent photographs and dictated autobiographical articles. An unexpected outcome was that a father entered an international Gypsy arts competition and won a prize. This had a very positive influence on his self-confidence and on that of his four children. One girl's poems won an award two years running and this may well have contributed to her decision and her parents' support for her to continue her education into the sixth form and beyond. Children in the feeder primary schools took part in the book project as a means of bridging the gap with secondary school and this provided their teachers with an an opportunity to talk with the parents.

Once the work on the book was completed, the children were invited to attend a youth club, initially for them and their friends. Again, the parents had to be consulted and the youth leader visited them in their homes to gain their approval. Another event was a family outing to the seaside, organised jointly by the community education and the Traveller teams. Activities such as these, with the strong backing of the school, have undoubtedly raised the Travellers' self-image, furthered co-operation between home and school, and greatly improved attendance.

Access to formal education is best promoted through continuous and regular attendance at school. However, this may at times be difficult or impossible for some Traveller pupils, for example those whose parents are showpeople or whose employment takes them outside Britain. Many schools now provide children with distance learning materials to help minimise the disruption caused by absence from school. Since the parents or relatives have to take responsibility for supervising their children's school work, it is essential for schools to prepare them carefully for the task. This is merely an extension of the work primary schools and special needs departments often do already, for example by running training sessions on paired reading.

While many showpeople have successfully supported the completion of their children's summer workpacks, it was believed that lower literacy levels among many Gypsies and other Travellers would make it impossible to set up distance learning programmes. Team members took part in an EC/DfE project on distance learning for this second group, with a focus on strategies for involving parents and other family members. The work was carried out in neighbouring primary schools in Cambridge, where children from large private sites travel for several months at a time in Germany, Belgium and the Netherlands. Mainstream and Traveller team teachers consulted parents about their perceived needs and worked together at home and in school to produce general guidance for other families, advice on how to share reading and develop literacy skills with their children, a pack of games and activities for parents to help children with early literacy and a set of practical science activities to complete at home. Most of the parents were anxious about their own reading capacities, so all the materials were also recorded on to short audio-cassettes. Parents were involved throughout in criticising and amending the materials and are now accustomed to requesting workpacks whenever they travel.

Concluding remarks

The respective viewpoints of Travellers and of schools may appear irreconcilable. Establishing common ground represents a considerable challenge. In the short term, Traveller education teams will have a continuing role, often acting as the first point of contact, finding ways to accommodate different opinions and raising awareness on both sides, but with the firm intention that one day they will be superfluous. When schools develop policies on home–school liaison, they need to consider specific strategies for ensuring that parents from all the local communities are included. There may be scope for all kinds of initiatives, such as offering employment in the school to Traveller parents, developing a family education project or involving non-Traveller parents in outreach. What is required is a flexible, practical and optimistic approach to a wide diversity of families and situations, together with the recognition that changing perceptions is a slow and cumulative task.

Notes

1. Section 36 of the 1944 Education Act states:

   It shall be the duty of the parent of every child of compulsory school age to cause him to receive efficient full-time education suitable to his age, ability and aptitude and to any special educational needs he may have either by regular attendance at school or otherwise.

   Some parents who choose to educate their children at home employ a private tutor or become members of 'Education Otherwise', an established voluntary organisation, which provides encouragement and practical support for around 10,000 families.

References

Council of Europe (1989a) The Council and the Ministers of Education meeting within the Council (22nd May) *School Provision for Children of Occupational Travellers.* Strasbourg: Council of Europe.

Council of Europe (1989b) The Council and the Ministers of Education meeting within the Council (22nd May) *School Provision for Gypsy and Traveller Children.* Strasbourg: Council of Europe.

DES (1967) *Children and their Primary Schools* (Plowden Report). London: HMSO.

DES (1983) *The Education of Travellers' Children.* HMI Discussion Paper. London: HMSO.

DES (1985) *Education for All: The Report of a Committee of Enquiry into the education of children from ethnic minority groups.* (Swann Report). London: HMSO.

DES (1990) Circular no. 10/90. London: HMSO.

DfEE (1996) *The Education of Travelling Children. A survey of educational provision for Travelling children.* London: OFSTED.

Li,gois, J-P. (1994) *Roma, Gypsies, Travellers.* Strasbourg: Council of Europe Press.

Reiss, C. (1975) *Education of Travelling Children: Schools Council Report.* London and Basingstoke: Macmillan.

Tizard, B., Mortimore, J. and Burchell, B. (1988) 'Involving Parents from Minority Groups', in Bastiani, J. *Parents and Teachers 2: From Policy to Practice.* Windsor: NFER-Nelson.

7 Raising attainment: home–school maths in a secondary multiethnic context

Alwyn Morgan and Jeremy Richardson

Involving parents, of any ethnic origin, in their children's education has never been the easiest of challenges for schools. This is despite the fact that the vast majority of parents want their children to do better, or most certainly as well as themselves.

There is generally speaking in the vast majority of homes, a healthy level of interest in their children's education, which is frequently displayed in the regular questioning of 'What did you do at school today?'. Sadly, young people do not respond particularly positively to such probing and frequently respond rather negatively, implying that they have done virtually nothing or 'not a lot'. Such a response does the parental perception of schooling a great disservice and also curtails the potential of any educational dialogue in the home. Over a period of time, parents are thus somewhat distanced from the educational experiences of their children, unless they make the positive commitment to become a parent helper and see for themselves the nature of current teaching practices. The occasional curriculum workshop for parents is rarely sufficient to rectify this matter. For some ethnic parents, discussing their children's schooling is an even greater challenge as they may not have experienced statutory schooling either in the UK or their own country of origin. For many parents what happens at school is therefore a considerable mystery.

Given the perceived level of parental support within most homes for children's education, it is sometimes perplexing for teachers to understand why this goodwill is not reflected in active support for activities planned specifically for parents. It is often noted that parents may support social or non-threatening activities but more formalised and curricular initiatives are frequently 'boycotted'.

In addition to the traditional invisible barriers that frequently surround schools, language, class and culture can often add to the encumbrance. Teachers who work in middle-class catchment areas will sometimes complain that parents are too demanding on matters relating to their children's education, while teachers who work in less advantaged areas often misinterpret the non-appearance of parents at school functions as apathy.

There are numerous reasons why parents do not display their active commitment to formalised parent functions. Some of the factors for this apparent minimal level of support include a lack of confidence or even a sense of intimidation in approaching teachers and schools, a fear that they have nothing to contribute, uneasiness about displaying any sense of ignorance, geographical isolation, lack of transport, the timing of such events and sometimes the belief that it is not their role to educate their children, etc. There are also other barriers that schools need to overcome in order to develop more effective links with ethnic parents. These include a sense of alienation from the system, the language barrier and related issues, the differing values to those of formal education. Additionally, there is also a lack of confidence in the educational process as there is a perception that it fails to lead to full-time permanent employment for their children.

Many schools, the majority of which are in the primary phase, are now actively seeking to address some of the above challenges – there is a traditional mistaken professional perception that parental involvement in children's education is solely an issue for primary schools and that when their children transfer to the secondary school, parents either are not interested, or their children do not want them to get involved. Working with parents in secondary schooling is therefore generally regarded as a very peripheral issue. Ethnic parents are therefore sometimes even more isolated from their children's schooling.

However, it cannot be imagined that parents stop caring about their children's education when they attain the age of eleven. Circumstances may change, but the parental commitment and goodwill remain. Many parents actively try to help their children at home but are frustrated over either not knowing what is taught or how to help and can be disenfranchised by the language and culture of the school.

The challenge to secondary schools and particularly those in either less advantaged areas or communities with a high percentage of mixed race is to harness the support and goodwill of parents. When parents are involved, the children will do better. The attitude and influence of the home can have quite a positive or negative impact on a child's aspirations in life. Sir Ron Dearing in his report *The National Curriculum and its Assessment* (Dearing 1994, para. 3.3) stated that:

> All involved with education recognise the great benefit to a child's progress that comes from the active support and involvement of parents ... Not all parents are themselves well equipped to offer assistance, but by showing strong interest in their child's achievements ... all parents can help greatly ... Parents must accept that the responsibility for the education of young children is one they share with the school: they handicap their child for life if they do not give the school the support the child needs to give of his or her best.

To respond to this challenge, schools need to take the initiative and seek pro-actively to develop imaginative and positive links with all parents, and particularly with those who may feel alienated from the educational system. One such school that is striving to respond in such a manner is Primrose

High School in Leeds – an inner city, multiethnic, eleven to eighteen comprehensive school with just over 560 pupils. Approximately 40 per cent of the pupils come from Bangladeshi homes and another 40 per cent from Pakistani homes. In September 1994, only 12 per cent of Year 7 pupils had a reading age of more than ten on entry to the school, with the average reading age being about eight years. Approximately 80 per cent of the pupils are entitled to free school meals.

There was little history of parental involvement, particularly through the curriculum. In fact there was a perception among some staff, that many of the values and aspirations held by the community were not particularly well aligned with those of the school. This situation was about to be changed.

In September 1993 a new headteacher was appointed, who sought to build on earlier links established with 'Leeds Education 2000' by the former headteacher. Primrose High School therefore remained one of seven schools in the Chapeltown, Harehills and Burmantoft areas of the city to be served by the Charitable Trust. Leeds Education 2000 is one of nine national projects affiliated to the work of 'Education 2000' nationally. This work is to campaign for a better understanding of how humans learn and how the education system can be redesigned accordingly with emphasis on involving every section of the community in the revitalisation of the learning process. John Abbott, the Director of 'Education 2000' nationally, also leads an international initiative which is concerned about the same issues.

One specific initiative at Primrose High School funded by Leeds Education 2000 was the employment of an educational consultant to involve the whole school staff in a process of raising awareness about community learning. The example of practice outlined in this chapter, was a major outcome of this contract.

The consultancy commenced in February 1994 with a training session for staff to raise awareness of the range of strategies that could be employed to work effectively with parents and the community. Specific emphasis was placed upon the role of parents as coeducators of their children. Two members of the maths department developed their interest in this issue by travelling to Humberside to attend a training course on IMPACT Maths – involving parents in their children's maths homework – an initiative developed by Professor Ruth Merttens at the University of North London.

The IMPACT or home school maths approach is based on the principle that the mathematical concept that is taught in school can be reinforced at home by means of a practical fun task or challenge. This might be a game, data collection exercise or a discussion activity, such as 'design an eyesight test'. All activities are selected to encourage and develop talking and listening within a mathematical context. Pupils therefore develop the language of hypothesis, making predictions, testing ideas, generalising, questioning, reporting and deducing. This approach demonstrates the relevance of the subject by utilising everyday mathematical situations. However, the most important principle underpinning these exercises is the assistance, support and discussion that is required from an older person to explore or debate the concept concerned.

However, while IMPACT maths has been embraced by ever increasing numbers of primary schools throughout the UK, secondary schools, for reasons best known to themselves, felt that 'it wasn't for them' Not so Primrose High School, who with financial support from Leeds Education 2000 decided that this approach to involving parents in their children's education had much to offer the school. Such a decision deserves admiration for the commitment and vision displayed in valuing the potential contribution that parents in this less advantaged inner-city area could make to their children's education. Many teachers might have felt that some parents with limited English and little experience of formal education, had little to contribute to their children's schooling.

Aims for the home–school maths approach were agreed in consultation with the school's three Curriculum and Parental Support Assistants (CPSAs), two of whom were Urdu speakers, the other Bengali. These proved to be key figures in the development of this work. The aims were as follows:

- to build a partnership with parents and carers in the mathematical education of their children;
- to create situations in the home which facilitate parent–child dialogue about mathematics and children's learning;
- to create parent/carer – teacher dialogue about mathematics and children's learning;
- to develop in pupils and parents a positive attitude towards mathematics in general;
- to develop in pupils a positive attitude towards mathematics homework;
- to raise levels of attainment in mathematics.

Having agreed on the aims, it was then decided to launch the scheme by arranging meetings for parents/carers. Meetings were planned for the Bangladeshi and Pakistani Centres and a local pub. However, the latter venue failed to materialise as it proved difficult to find a suitable meeting room. This meeting was subsequently held at school. Prior to the two sessions in the local community centres, meetings were arranged with the community leaders who welcomed the school's initiative and made practical suggestions for the timing and management of the meetings. Additionally, the CPSAs and members of the maths department home visited all Year 7 parents to explain the aims of the work and provide details on the 'launch' meetings. Parents also received letters in their mother tongues to remind them of the meetings.

Each meeting followed the same format and was split into three parts. Firstly, there was a ten-minute introduction from the head of maths, which was translated by a CPSA. Several points were stressed, namely:

- the notion of partnership – children spend more time at home than at school;
- how parents can help their children learn – giving instruction, asking questions and listening;

- the nature of 'modern' maths – fun, encouraging children to develop their own methods, estimation and mental calculation and the 'new' topics of data handling and probability.

Following this, parents were invited to work on IMPACT activities with their children. This proved very popular – the children soon helped the parents to get over their initial anxieties and embarrassments. There were initial concerns over the language demands of the tasks but these soon proved to be unwarranted as the pupils explained the challenge to their parents, who then completed the necessary activities together, through the medium of their mother tongue. Time was also given over to the completion of homework diaries by parents and pupils. This proved to be an invaluable mechanism for developing the working relationship between home and school.

The meetings drew to a close with an explanation from the school on the practical detail on how the scheme would be operated. This was followed by time for questions. At the community centre meetings, the local community leaders urged parents to appreciate what the school was trying to do and to make sure that they undertook the tasks with their children. On the suggestion of parents certain phrases and mathematical terminology was translated and placed in the pupils' homework diaries during their Urdu and Bengali lessons. In total, approximately 60 per cent of the parents attended these 'launch' meetings.

Following this series of meetings, the mathematics department decided upon a fixed day and time when all Year 7 pupils would have their IMPACT lesson. This would be when the new task for the week would be explained and the previous week's task would be discussed and developed. Parents were also invited to participate in this lesson. Whilst the average attendance varied between three and four, this proved to be a significant development in the school's home–school liaison strategy. It brought teachers, pupils and parents to work together on mathematical challenges. It also built upon the school's existing commitment to be open and welcoming to parents.

The homework diaries became an integral feature of the work. These provided the opportunity for parents and pupils to comment on the nature of the homework and state whether it was too easy, too hard or just about right. Space was also provided for further comment between the home and teacher. These booklets provided teachers with an insight into who worked with the pupils. Many pupils worked not with a parent or carer but with an older brother, sister or relative. It also gave the school an insight into the mathematical experience and confidence of the person who worked with the pupil. Some would write comments like, 'I enjoyed it, it was good'. Others would comment that, 'I showed Ikram how to work out surface area using the formula $A = L * B$. I explained in which aspects he can use this theory'. Other comments provided an insight into parental perceptions and expectations of mathematics homework, 'Guess who had to put the toys away again! Great fun this one. What should we have learned?' Other comments provided the opportunity to assist parents and carers to teach their children mathematics e.g. 'Farhat did her homework with her sister playing. Had difficulty trying to show her how to set it out. Let her do it her own way in the end'. On reflection the diaries became a small 'record of achievement', genuinely shared between parent/carer, child and teacher. The quality of the dialogue and the ensuing working relationship between home and school became one of the most powerful outcomes of this work. This newly established inter-reaction with the home also made parents' evenings far more effective by enabling both parties to plunge into the mathematical issues facing the child in question.

This approach to the teaching of mathematics also assisted to change pupils' perception of the subject and particularly maths homework. Pupils became very enthusiastic about IMPACT maths and would enquire whether they could have an IMPACT lesson. Older siblings would also question why they couldn't have similar homework.

This work also encouraged family members to give each other quality time. One pupil, when questioned about the benefits of the work, stated that generally speaking, she did not see much of her father. As she came home from school, he would be going to bed. However, when there was an IMPACT homework he would stay up and complete the challenges with his daughter. Once these were completed, he would devise similar tasks for them both to complete. In an age when there are so many distractions that take individual members of families in their own separate directions, the home's involvement with homework brings a variety of rewards.

At the end of the first term, a letter of thanks was sent to all Year 7 parents as an expression of thanks for their support and also to request views on how the home school maths scheme could be improved. A number of parents who had been particularly helpful were also personally invited to discuss the development of the work. Following the end of the second term, consultation meetings were held with parents in the community centres and school. These were held during the day. Attendance was poor and did not truly reflect the degree of involvement that was forthcoming from the parents.

The IMPACT/home–school mathematics scheme has now been operational for just over twelve months and the Department has identified several issues that need to be addressed. These are as follows:

- There is a need for more thorough integration of the activities into the department's scheme of work. Initially, the prime concern was parental partnership, with the suitability of the tasks in terms of appropriateness in the context of the other work being less important. Now that the scheme of work is well established with pupils and parents, the homework activities will be integrated more closely into established schemes of work.
- The language demands of some of the challenges require to be addressed. Considerable time has been spent in class explaining to

pupils the role expected of parents or carers. This takes away from the time allocated for follow-up work from the previous week's activity. The department wishes to produce tasks and challenges that will help parents/carers to develop their English within the context of mathematics.

- Differentiation – although many of the tasks are differentiated by outcome, there is a need to set tasks that fully test, challenge and motivate all pupils.
- Development – strategies are now being considered to extend the work into the whole of Key Stage 3. Encouragingly, pupils, parents and teachers have all expressed an interest in exploring more substantial tasks that may be worked on for a few weeks or even half a term.

There is much to be looked forward to.

While it is abundantly clear that the IMPACT/home–school maths scheme is achieving its aims, even within such a short time scale, there has been no formal evaluation of this work to date. This will continue to be a target, pending the availability of funding.

Informal feedback received by the maths department has been as follows:

From pupils

Very popular – pupils love it. Homework handing in rate is very high right across the ability range. Pupils in other year groups are jealous, and often ask if they can do IMPACT. Brothers and sisters higher up the school who help their siblings are impressed and talk to their teachers about it.

From parents

Parents have found children more willing to do their homework because it's more fun. They think it is important for their children and should continue in other years. They like the problem-solving approach of many of the activities though some felt that there should be more traditional 'sums'. They feel it involves them much more in what happens in school and their children's education. It encourages them to make the effort to help their children.

There are also numerous wider benefits for the school that will be clearly evident to all readers. However, the greatest lesson for all concerned, is that homes where the mother tongue might not be English are quite capable of becoming involved in not only their children's mathematical education, but also in the wider experiences of the whole curriculum. If the support and involvement of the home is forthcoming for mathematics, a subject that strikes fear into many adults, opportunities must abound for imaginative teachers to broaden this approach into other curricular subjects. As and when such a situation arises, schools may more readily start using the term 'partnership with parents'. Additionally, the 'shared responsibility' for children's education suggested by Sir Ron Dearing may slowly become a reality. Most importantly, when parents have a clearer insight into what their children are being taught and how they can help their children at home, standards of attainment will undoubtedly be raised.

The transferability of this good practice to other schools will be dependent on the ability of interested parties to match certain principles noted in the work at Primrose High School. These include:

- The willingness of teachers to value the contribution that all parents can make to their children's education, irrespective of their background, class, language or culture. All too often many professionals fail to appreciate the commitment and goodwill within the home for children's education. Sadly there may be a minority of teachers who feel that parents do not have the capability or interest to help their children. While some may be able to do it better than others, opportunities need to be provided to generate a culture of partnership for young people's education. Additionally, the professionally held myth of parental 'apathy' needs to be dispelled. Could it be that schools need to examine more closely why certain functions arranged for parents are poorly attended?
- Where there may be a reluctance or inability on the part of parents to visit the school, there is merit in meeting parents on their home territory. In this particular case the meetings held in the local community centres and the home visiting programme paid substantial dividends. For other more formalised parents' meetings which need to be held at Primrose High School, the staff will run a minibus service for those parents in need of assistance with transport. This is much appreciated by the parents.
- The mother tongue needs to be valued and utilised and be seen as an asset and not a problem. In this particular case the intermediary role fulfilled by the curriculum and parent support assistants was a key factor in assisting to win the goodwill and support of parents and their community leaders. Additionally, they also ensured that all written communication was sent to the homes in the pupils' mother tongue. Most importantly, the homework challenges were actively encouraged to be undertaken through the language of the home.
- Once the goodwill and commitment of the home had been secured, it was nurtured and appreciated as demonstrated with the letters of thanks and the consultation regarding the development of the home–school maths work. Relationships need to be of a two-way nature and partners need to feel that they are not taken for granted. Sadly, in the past, schools' links with parents have sometimes had a notorious tendency to be rather one-sided with constant expectations of the parents to give and support, with little being given back in return.
- Training teachers to work with parents played an important role in winning the initial commitment of the mathematics department to consider

the IMPACT maths work. Sadly, few teachers have been trained to work with parents, which accounts for why many schools and their teaching staff continue to regard parents as a peripheral issue. While this situation remains unchanged, schools are failing to capitalise on one of their most valued resources.

• Finally and most importantly, there must be a commitment by the school's management to make such an approach a reality. Without such support, work of this nature is a non-starter. There are substantial policy implications for the school. This matter has been readily forthcoming at Primrose High School.

In conclusion three points can be made. Firstly, in addition to the numerous benefits that this work brings to Primrose High School, its parents and pupils, it also meets the new *OFSTED Guidance on the Inspection of Secondary Schools* (1995, para 5.5), namely that inspectors must evaluate and report on, 'parents' involvement with the work of the school and with their children's work at home ... Judgements should be based on the extent to which ... links with parents contribute to children's learning'. There should be no conflict of opinion on this particular point.

Secondly, as stated earlier, the practice outlined in this chapter illustrates quite clearly that parents of ethnic background are very willing and able to help their children at home. Teachers need to value and give parents the opportunity to get involved.

However, the final point is the key feature of the entire process, namely, the nature of the maths homework challenges. It is essential that they are interesting and suitably challenging to catch the imagination of all parents and pupils. They must generate a genuine need for an educational dialogue between the child and helper. The tasks then become the vehicle for working together, which, in turn, bring into place all the other features of this work. All concerned really must want to talk about the task or homework challenge.

Involving parents in homework therefore transcends the often professionally perceived issues of language, class, culture and all other barriers that surround schools. This approach can also be adapted for any curriculum subject. When home and school collaborate in this manner, it does have an impact on standards of attainment.

References

Dearing, R. (1994) *The National Curriculum and its Assessment*, December. London: School Curriculum and Assessment Authority.
OFSTED (1995) *Guidance on the Inspection of Secondary Schools*. London: HMSO.

8 The interrupted learner: whose responsibility?

Elizabeth Jordan and Pat Holmes

Discontinuity in learning

The state school system has been developed for a largely static population, so much so that even the transition from nursery to primary school and from primary to secondary is seen to be a major upheaval in a pupil's education. Much research has been directed at uncovering the factors which support or detract from a smooth and happy transition. Yet, little research is undertaken on other forms of discontinuity in learning.

Part of the problem lies with the fact that all schools share the common experience of the transition stages, but far fewer experience, or acknowledge, the particular needs of the interrupted learner. At least, that is the generally perceived picture: but if one considers the full range of pupils who experience discontinuity, then such a perception should be challenged.

Table 8.1

Provision	Client group(s)
Usual provision	Settled population
the school staff/pupil ratio set classes	Settled population short breaks for illness, holidays, exclusions
Extra provision usually provided by EA	

support staff
special tutorials
     class
     units
hospital school
home tuition
ESL
Traveller teachers
	learning difficulties, including dyslexia
	special needs, physical and
	sensory impairments
	
	chronic sick and long-term sick
	phobics and long-term sick
	bilingual learners
	Gypsy Travellers and occupational Travellers

Further needs in learning subject to special funding	
home–school link-teaching home–school tutorial support home–school ODL	pregnant schoolgirls disaffected pupils – exclusions, truants main carers of sick adults highly mobile families – B & B – Travellers

Every school accepts that pupils will be absent for some periods because of normal childhood illnesses and generally tutoring is provided on return so that pupils catch up with their peer group. Where a pupil requires more extended absence, usually as a result of an accident or a family holiday, work is provided to do at home with the support of the parents and, on return to school, tutoring may be provided on an ad hoc basis. These approaches are standard and considered normal. Even so, such absences are still felt to be threatening to pupils' progress and parents are often made to feel guilty at daring to take a family holiday in term time. For increasing numbers of people holiday dates are set by the employers and for the Showman's community holidays can only be taken in the non-working period, i.e. when they are in the winter school.

For those other groups of pupils who will have time out from the daily routines of school there may be less on offer and in many cases less sympathy, for instance, school refusers, truants, pregnant girls. The pupil is very much at the mercy of what the individual school can, or rather, feels it is able to offer. There is no right to receive education out of school. The dilemma for parents is that there seems only to be 'a place in school' on offer so that any absence from that 'place in school' is, in a sense, seen as a dereliction of the parental obligation, as evidenced in the furore over absenteeism and truancy figures. In recent years performance league tables in National Curricula and associated tests and exams have exacerbated the pressure on parents to ensure that their child attends school regularly. Yet, paradoxically, parents who do send a sick child back to school too soon are viewed by the school staff as selfish and uncaring.

For some parents coping with both the family's needs and the education system's demands creates tensions that can lead to the development of negative attitudes on both sides, such as families forced to live in bed and breakfast accommodation who are constantly being moved, mobile Travellers and ethnic groups who make extended return visits to 'home' land.

The exclusive system

It is important to discriminate between the system and the individual school; most schools are very caring and try to do the best they can within the degrees of flexibility they have. This flexibility is the key factor in how effective schools are at meeting the needs of the interrupted learner (Mortimore *et al.* 1988). The standard organisational set up of staff/pupil ratios and timetabled classes, etc., leaves little room for flexibility in accommodating the needs of pupils who depart from the perceived norm.

It is this concept of norm which underpins much of the inherent discrimination in the education system. The parental role in supporting the pupils' learning is widely acknowledged and some steps have been taken to give them their place. But, it can be argued that the place they have been given is merely one of supporting the established cultural mores of the school world and reinforcing the values disseminated through the school curriculum. Any dissension from that role poses a threat; parents are marked as uncooperative or even uncaring of their children. Diversity in race, gender and disability are given support (albeit on occasions only tacit) but diversity in the degree of value ascribed to regular attendance is not tolerated. The evidence to support this is to be found in the lack of available alternatives to full attendance.

What is there then available for those parents who need to have their children out of school for periods during the school session? The evidence is that official responses are patchy. Local authorities generally make some limited provision for the chronically ill, the school refusers or truants and the under-age pregnant, but there is little evidence to suggest that the level of support to the families involved is other than minimal and very much dependent on the level of local provision, which can vary enormously. For parents struggling with the associated emotional and time-consuming problems the added burden of ensuring their child gets the necessary coherent educational experience is rightly seen by the public as unfair but is passed off as the result of inadequacy in resources. For those others, who because of cultural life styles cannot ensure full attendance at one school, it is not accepted as 'unfair', but rather it is seen to be the fault of the parents. The education system does not support such diversity of opinion; it is seen as deviance.

It is ironic that at post-school level there is already full acknowledgment of the diversity in learners' needs and flexible learning units have been developed in most Further Education colleges, with a plethora of open learning courses devised, even for those with few literacy or study skills. Colleges and universities, traditionally viewed as exclusive institutions because of their selection processes, are now leading the way in supporting the intermittent attender and in meeting the learning needs of a wide diversity in ability, culture and gender.

Why then does school education remain so discriminatory? It may be that the clients' needs are not considered in the way that they are at post-school level. While the ministers for education control the finance and general policy governing all sectors in education, the degree of control over staffing and curriculum is far tighter and more prescribed at school level. The result is that ensuring conformity to a narrow pattern of options is seen to be far more important than ensuring that all pupils, whatever their family situation and circumstances, do become supported learners, confident in the likelihood of success and able to reach their full potential.

Travellers' needs in state education

For most of this century there has been some protection from prosecution for their children's absence from school while the family is legitimately travelling for work purposes. Legislation varies within the different areas of the UK, but in general, Travellers are expected to accumulate a minimum of at least 200 attendances, i.e. 100 school days, in a session.

If we agree that parents are the first educators of their children it follows that they teach from their own experience. Traditionally, the Gypsy and Traveller families have operated in extended family units as mobile 'self-employed' labour forces, undertaking work in which the whole family could participate. Children have been seen as trainee adults, to be inducted from an early age into the family work. They have learned through emulation, undertaking adult tasks alongside adult members of the family and supervised by them. It has not been their experience, therefore, to learn first through play and then later transfer what has been learned to real tasks or situations, as is thought usual within the settled community.

The strength and viability of the travelling communities have been their ability to adapt to meet changing economic circumstances and challenges. Mechanisation of farming in the 1950s and 1960s, combined with new land and planning legislation drove hundreds of families out of the rural areas and into urban conurbation in pursuit of new work opportunities, in scrap metal collecting, road making, tarmaccing, and trading in carpets, furniture, etc. This in turn brought changes within the family; in some instances such work opportunities were for male members only. For many families these changes have meant that there is no longer a family business to induct all of the children into. Now, in the 1990s, with the steel industry having been scaled down, scrap metal collection and recycling, for instance, provide only a modest living for very few families, so again new opportunities are being sought.

Site accommodation provision is now no longer an obligation on local authorities and planning permission to live or build on land that belongs to the family is not easy to achieve. As a result many families have no legal place to stay and have to move on from one unauthorised camp to another, always risking prosecution as criminal trespassers under the Criminal Justice and Public Order Act, 1994. Families who have managed to get a pitch on a local authority site now see their children having to move off the site when they become independent and marry as there are no spare pitches available for them. Consequently, the young people have to leave for an existence on the roadside, operating without the usual close support of the extended family and often without the necessary skills which the parents and grand-parents had for living on the roadside without basic amenities to hand. Young mothers now find themselves engaged in twenty-four-hour child care, which is alien to them, coming from an extended family situation where shared care is predominant. Some fear for their children's safety living in such dangerous surroundings, with the result that the children are restrained in chairs or pushchairs within the trailer rather than let free outside on the waste ground they have to camp on. For some children this care for their safety has resulted in delay in their development in terms of gross motor movement, spatial awareness, etc.

As a result of their mobility the parent group have little or no experience of schooling; those few who have often had negative and hostile experiences. Knowledge of schooling is usually limited to reading and writing with occasionally maths, hence parental expectations of what schools have to offer are narrow.

But many parents are now realising that if they are to remain independent, viable and competitive as a distinct community in the future, they will have to ensure that their children acquire new formal skills to add to the family taught skills. They will need access to schooling, but one which does not require that they leave their ethnic or cultural values at the school door.

Creating equality of opportunities in state education

In England and Wales a specific grant has been made available to LEAs since 1990 through the Section 210 funding arrangements from the Department for Education and Employment (DfEE) to support some degree of flexibility in response at local authority level for Travellers in England and Wales. The thrust of such support has been to provide teams of teachers to support Traveller access into schools and to help ensure some degree of continuity and coherence in their education as they travel. In other areas individual education authorities have supported a variety of responses to Travellers' needs at a local level, usually through visiting support teaching staff.

Partnerships in education are being promoted at all levels: in supporting the interrupted learner they are vital. Unlike an independent and mature adult learner a child does need constant regular feedback from adults in order to make progress. For many young Travellers this feedback is met through the Traveller Education Support Service (TESS) staff who have developed a well-integrated support network across local education authorities. Where this system breaks down is where there is no such flexible team available or where the level of staffing in a TESS is inadequate to serve all the pupils in that area. It has the added drawback, as with all external support mechanisms, that it can also implicitly encourage schools to abnegate their responsibility for the Traveller pupils. Such a separate system promises little hope of ever ensuring equality of opportunity in education within schools for Travellers unless it operates in a fully integrated partnership with schools. Fortunately, there are now many teams working in close partnership with schools to help meet Traveller pupils' needs in the same way that generic learning support or special needs support staff do to prevent learning difficulties arising through inappropriate curriculum demands.

Inevitably, given the high level of non-attendance patterns, the work of the support teams has focused on families rather than individual children. This close partnership approach has raised awareness in staff of the very real needs of the families. For parents who have had little or no schooling themselves it is no easy task to make demands on a state system. Staff have had to provide information and give support to parents in broadening their knowledge so that they have come increasingly to appreciate and demand their rights while trying to carry out their responsibilities for the education of their children.

A significant factor in enabling parents to access schooling has been the authority initiatives aimed at supporting Gypsy Traveller youngsters in schools, usually in co-operation with community education and other local-based education services. However, one of the salutary lessons from such work has been that while many Travellers can be seen to be victims within this society because of the high degree of prejudice and discrimination accorded them, they are by no means all victims in the sense of being dependent on others for their survival or wellbeing. TESS staff have had to learn to temper their desire to speak up for the Travelling communities so that they do not inculcate learned dependency in the parents: it is only too easy for professionals to develop a reliance on the permanence of their 'victim' group, they are their *raison d'être* after all.

Yet, how else are schools to change, to be able to increase their flexibility in organisation and methodology, if they are not an active partner with the TESS? The experiential learning that the Traveller teachers have derived through working out of schools and with families is proving invaluable. For instance, it is inappropriate to deal with the child in isolation; the child's educational needs must be considered within the context of the family unit as it is given such a high status in their cultures. Any work that is given to the pupil to complete out of school must fit in with the family circumstances, i.e. level of family literacy, space for writing and storage of books, access to libraries, relevance to cultural mores and values, time demands, language differences, as in the case of circus families where each parent, grandparent and other close relative may have a wide variety of 'home' languages. Most Travelling families move for work purposes so that finding regular set aside time to devote to helping the child with school work is difficult to organise. At other times travelling may be to participate in an extended family or cultural event; set aside time on those occasions is also problematic. Where families have come to see the benefits of regular periods of learning with a teacher, they increasingly take responsibility for ensuring that it also happens while travelling. Many families now regularly contact the support services themselves to seek resources and tuition, to return completed work for marking and feedback and for contact and support. Responses from providers have to be immediate, given the transitory nature of the travelling life, and appropriate in their terms to ensure that the learning tasks will be undertaken.

Where Travellers' movements are planned and communicated to teaching staff some continuity can be arranged. Unfortunately, the movement of some groups is more likely to be due to enforced eviction, which is erratic and undermining of family security. The impact of the disruption of enforced movement, often over short distances, can be lessened through the provision of transport to maintain the children in the same school despite the 'home' movement. This enables continuity and stability, not only in their education, but against a background of stressful imposed disruption for the whole family. For families in these circumstances their choices in education are limited and often dependent on TESS to support access and continuity.

Seasonal travelling by showmen who leave their winter yards in March and tour until November requires a different educational response as their children regularly attend schools local to the winter quarters during the winter period. The families regard these base schools as 'theirs' and are loyal to them. Some schools do send work with the children in the hope that they will not regress educationally during the long absence. Support services help them keep in touch with their schools and give direct help to enable the children to keep up with their peers while travelling.

A growing number of young parents today have themselves experienced primary education and have had the support of TESS staff. In turn they are now seeking preschool experiences for their children and entering them into primary school independently. So far this has not been the experience at secondary level in any great numbers so that transfer and maintenance support is now the focus of development and support. It may be some time before the achievements in access and increased attendance seen at primary level will be repeated at secondary and probably only then if the same high level of care is afforded to parents and children as participants and stake holders in the process rather than having it 'done to them'. Increased direct relevance of curriculum at secondary level is essential since Travellers are practical and pragmatic people. Flexibility in terms of courses followed, in the variety of marking and assessment opportunities, especially in terms of when and where exams can be taken, are all key issues for youngsters who travel if schooling and formal education are to become meaningful activities for them.

Home–school links

The right to ethnicity and the right to travel necessitates schools working with the parents and children to maximise their educational opportunities. Acceptance is not enough without clear aims and practical actions for successful outcomes. Even for children living permanently on local authority or private sites or in housing, distance between home and school can still exist if the history, traditions and cultures of the community are not known or valued by the school and the parents do not know or understand the values and expectations of the schools. It is important not to assume anything about parents' knowledge of the education system or schools. It is necessary to be prepared to discuss how schools work, how learning takes place, the cumulative effects of formal learning, the need to practice skills in order to ensure mastery, the need for pupil records and their purpose, the parents' role in aiding their transfer to the next school and what they can do to support their children's learning. All this has to be transmitted regularly and orally as Travellers are often not literate. This process must be sensitive and supportive of their self esteem. It is important, therefore, to listen to them; their child is with you on trust.

Schools with proactive home–school policies and practice, or schools which work closely with TESS, endeavour to use outreach strategies to meet parents in the security of their own environment. They work to build a shared understanding of parent and school expectations because the interests of the child is at the heart of the liaison process. They acknowledge the demands of the travelling year, recognise and work to ameliorate the home and school calendars' clash, to help ensure that children do not miss out on primary/secondary school transfer visits, choosing subject options at secondary level, booking for autumn field trips, careers guidance and school and national assessment and examination arrangements. For Traveller pupils it is important to be able to sit exams at an alternative centre near to where they may be at that time. This does mean that home and school must co-operate well in advance to make the necessary arrangements.

Far greater expectations of education can be encouraged when parents are given access to the learning process and see their children making progress within it. Schools spending time constructively in resolving areas they are finding difficult are far preferable to the waste of time invested in managing symptoms of alienation and disaffection.

Distance learning for equality of opportunity

The need for support to ensure equality of opportunity in education is recognised by the Commission of the European Union which prioritises the needs of Gypsies and Occupational Travellers, intercultural education and distance learning within the SOCRATES programme. Bids are invited from all EU countries, working in transnational partnerships, to enable new and creative solutions to be developed and tested before implementation proper.

Current projects in the UK, including those coordinated by the National Association of Teachers of Travellers (NATT) and the European Federation for the Education of Children of Occupational Travellers (EFECOT), focus on the development of flexible learning strategies. These include:

- distance learning;
- differentiating the curriculum into attractive packages;
- using new technology, including innovative support and delivery with mobile phones, CDI using radio band, fax tutoring;
- opportunities to increase competence in developing school-based dis-

tance learning through the provision of guidelines and a staff development pack, *What is your school doing for Traveller children?* (EFECOT 1995) (O'Hanlon 1996).

While not strictly a legal duty of the schools, it is a method of ensuring that the children return to school in the winter engaged with the curriculum and the class work, feeling comfortable socially about their ability to work alongside their peers. Formerly, without this provision, increasing gaps in achievement between them and their peers with each successive travel period resulted in disaffection at an early age; withdrawal symptoms or difficult behaviour had to be managed in the classroom and school drop out was not uncommon.

The use of distance learning approaches has meant that some children are learning progressively now, rather than simply being prevented from educational regression. To learn independently children need to have the necessary resources within themselves; they need a basic level of literacy, self-study techniques, a degree of interest and motivation and a belief in themselves as learners. Parents, too, have to have awareness of what is involved for the child and their own particular role in supporting home, or distance learning. Advice for parents includes:

- ensuring a regular time for school work;
- building a habit of not allowing children out until the daily work is completed;
- providing a quiet space, e.g. a work top, with a chair;
- ensuring that the TV, audio-cassettes and younger siblings do not disturb (this is very difficult in the limited space available to them);
- making supportive responses, such as: 'that is very neat', 'you have done well', 'read it to me now', 'if you can't do it, let's talk about it and make a note of it so that you can ask for help'.

Although it has been easier to implement distance learning with the showmen's families, due to their fairly well-established routines in travelling and annual return to the base school, this work is now being extended to Gypsy children, some of whom are currently travelling and working as far away as Germany and Denmark. Distance learning has been operating even at this distance, although the best examples of successful work are those which are monitored regularly by TESS and schools as they travel within the UK. Still in its infancy, distance learning teaching skills and quality are improving year by year, but the level of support tuition as they travel is still sometimes patchy and very dependent on what is available in whichever area they find themselves.

Security of additional funding to support this national initiative will continue to be essential to allow the process of including minorities who have historically been excluded from formal education. There is an urgent need for funding to ensure consistency in provision and practice as families do move the length and breadth of the UK. Inconsistency leads to lowered expectations which can be highly damaging, particularly at critical periods in the family's progress into schooling. Despite excellent work at all levels, the culture and practice of schools is slow to change to accommodate the particular needs of Travellers. TESS have and are continuing to be key players in this change process.

Travellers cannot afford to have another generation miss out on the advantages that education brings. This is brought home most clearly now that it is mandatory to complete a written test as part of the driving test. For an oral culture that relies on wheels for the maintenance of livelihood and culture, it is now essential to have access to a full education; to miss out is to become further disadvantaged and marginalised.

References

EFECOT (1995) *What is Your School Doing for Traveller Children?: guidelines on good practice*. Plymouth: EFECOT.

Jordan, E. and Carroll, L. (1994) *Attendance Patterns of Showground Children in 4 Secondary Schools in Glasgow*. Edinburgh: Moray House Institute of Education.

Mortimore, P., Sammons, P. and Stone, L. (1988) *School Matters: the junior years*. Somerset: Open Books.

NATT (1995) *Education Contacts for Travelling Families*, 1995/96.

OFSTED (1996) *The Education of Travelling Children. A report from the office of Her Majesty's Chief Inspector of Schools*. London: HMSO.

O'Hanlon, C. (1996) *What is Your School Doing for Traveller Children?: a staff development pack*. Plymouth: EFECOT.

STEP (1993) *Education: your rights and responsibilities*. Edinburgh: SCF.

9 Meeting the needs of dual heritage children

Latika Davis and Rachel Evans

Introduction

As professionals and parents in Coventry, we have come in to contact with children of dual heritage who have a wide range of experiences and self-images; some are very positive about their dual heritage, some are indifferent and some have had negative experiences and have a negative self-image. Children with positive self-identify and high self-esteem are confident learners with high achievement. We want all children to attain this.

In our work our aims have been:

- to raise awareness of school staff to issues concerning pupils of dual heritage;
- to promote and contribute to good practice in meeting individual pupil's needs and ensuring that all pupils receive their entitlement in education and develop a positive self-image;
- to enable parents and carers of dual heritage children;
- to discuss strategies for developing positive self-image.

The importance of working in a positive way to encourage familiarity and acceptance of all aspects of a child's heritage is vital to the development of a positive self-image in any child. For most children, living with their birth families, information about and access to their heritage is part of everyday life, and this may be equally true for a child of dual heritage. In some cases, however, such children may only learn about and have access to their 'white' heritage even though they are usually perceived by society as 'black' (with all the accompanying implications) and this can lead to difficulties in terms of identity and self-esteem. Their only perceptions of black heritage and black identity may be obtained through negative media portrayal; they may not even be aware that other people perceive them as black until someone 'tells' them. We have been encouraging professionals, parents and carers to consider the role they may play in addressing some of these issues and enabling children to explore all aspects of their heritage, thus supporting the development of a positive identity.

Focus

For the purposes of the work undertaken in Coventry we have focused on children of dual heritage whose origin is a combination of the ethnic groups shown in Figure 9.1.

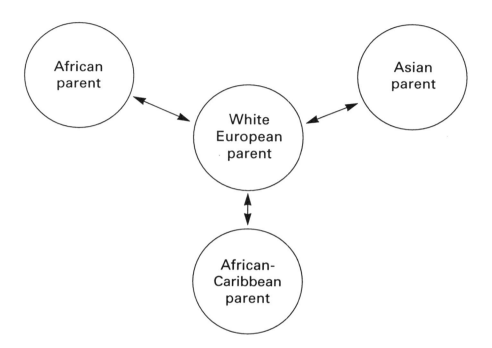

Figure 9.1 Dual heritage combinations

   While we recognise that the term dual heritage can be applied to a far broader section of the population e.g. English/French, Hindu/Sikh Indian/Chinese dual heritage, etc., we felt that they were less likely to involve the same complexity of issues in terms of ethnicity and culture. This does not mean that we ignore their experiences, and it is likely that many of the issues we raise might be the same for them as for our focus group.

Terminology

It is important to recognise the rights of individuals to decide what to call themselves, and one issue for us has been terminology. There have been and still are many different ways of describing children who have one 'white' and one 'black' parent. As a team, we discussed our views on the various terms listed in Figure 9.2.

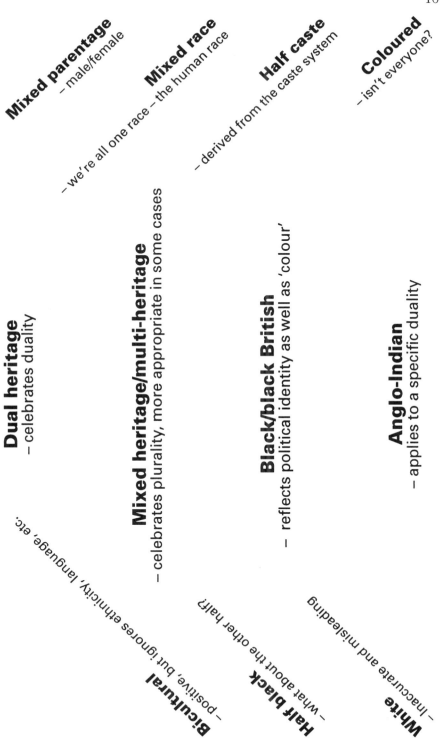

Figure 9.2 Terminology

Mixed parentage
– male/female

Mixed race
– we're all one race – the human race

Half caste
– derived from the caste system

Coloured
– isn't everyone?

Dual heritage
– celebrates duality

Mixed heritage/multi-heritage
– celebrates plurality, more appropriate in some cases

Black/black British
– reflects political identity as well as 'colour'

Anglo-Indian
– applies to a specific duality

Bicultural
– positive, but ignores ethnicity, language, etc.

Half black
– what about the other half?

White
– Inaccurate and misleading

A person's heritage is that which is passed down to them and includes attitudes, beliefs and experiences, as well as physical, tangible things. The term 'dual heritage' is the preferred term of the team who feel it is positive, allowing us to focus on the broader issues of identity and acknowledging the duality of a child's potential in terms of the resources from which they can draw strength. However, we accept that others may choose different terminology and believe that one person's preferred terms should never be forced upon another person. It is important that people are not chastised for using the 'wrong' term, but are provided with opportunities to explore what they mean by the label they use. For a child to suddenly be told they are 'black' when they have previously been told they are 'mixed race', or vice versa, may cause confusion. For a parent or carer to be told that the language they use is 'wrong' may make them defensive and affect their own confidence. We believe that terminology should not become an issue in itself but that a discussion about labels, where they come from and what they mean, can be useful for developing shared identity and understanding.

The work

We started by having an informal discussion between minority group support service staff and school colleagues many of whom, like us, are also parents within dual-heritage families. Following our initial discussion we have held workshops in schools and at conferences involving adults who work with and/or live in dual-heritage families.

Within our workshops we have used various quotes from professionals, parents and children to facilitate discussion of the issues e.g:

1. 'I'm not black or white. I'm brown and I'm glad.'
2. 'I get presents at Diwali and Christmas.'
3. 'My child is not half anything, she's twice as good.'
4. 'Slam in the yam with the lamb, mam.'
5. 'Mummy, why am I the only black person here?' (at a family gathering)
6. 'The only problem children in my school are the mixed race children.'
7. 'All our children are the same, we don't treat them differently.'
8. 'Shall I put them down as 'White other' then?'
9. 'All dual-heritage children should be regarded as black.'
10. 'No one ever told me I was black.'

The responses to these quotes have been fascinating in their variety. For example, one person may see quote 2 as positive, indicating a positive integration of two different faiths. Another person may envisage a child living in a state of confusion and yet another person may see a child simply 'showing off' about a material fact without necessarily having any deeper understanding of either faith. Clearly therefore the quote illustrates the need to treat children individually; the same statement from different children may have entirely different meaning and implication, depending on the context. This particular child was being materialistic, but also taking her dual heritage for granted.

Quotes 9 and 10 are in many ways two sides of the same important coin for some dual heritage children. Quote number 9 has formed part of many institutional policies and as such is crucial in the interaction of a family with these institutions. Quote number 10 may be the contrasting reality for some children, and it is important therefore to ensure that children's previous perceptions of themselves are not invalidated in their interaction with institutions. Care, support and a non-judgemental attitude are needed as children come to their own recognition of themselves.

To enable further exploration, not only of the issues involved but also of strategies that could be used to support children in varying situations, we have used 'positive' and 'negative' case studies, some examples of which are below.

Case study 1

A seven-year-old dual-heritage pupil lives with both of his parents and attends a multiethnic school. At school he plays only with 'white' children. For his birthday parties he only invites children with blond hair and fair skin. When asked to choose his favourite characters in books, he always chooses white characters.

Adults who observe this child need to acknowledge that the child may see himself as white and have negative perceptions about black people. Communication between home and school about his behaviour is important to build a comprehensive picture, as in isolation each party may not realise the seriousness of the situation. Busy teachers often only talk to parents when there is a serious behaviour/achievement problem. This particular child may appear to be well socialised until both parties share their knowledge. Once they have recognised the issue, they need to discuss their strategies to deal with it.

The child's parents need to provide opportunities for the child to celebrate his black heritage. The school needs to look at its broad and 'hidden' curriculum to ensure that it reflects the cultural, ethnic and linguistic diversity of its population. The class teacher needs to look at the personal and social education programme to ensure that it enables all the pupils to explore their own identities in a positive way. It is important to tackle the issue slowly and carefully and not simply focus the discussion on one individual child.

Case study 2

A mainly white school has to return ethnicity data to the Department of Education and Employment. The school records on ethnicity have not been completed by all families. The class teacher decides that because a ten-year-old dual-heritage pupil lives with her white mum and looks almost white, she should be in the 'European/White' category. In the playground, some white children call the dual-heritage pupil racist names such as 'paki' and 'coconut'.

The lack of awareness of racial bullying in the playground, and the lack of concern about consultation with parents are serious issues that need to be tackled by the whole school. Ten year olds are beginning to develop their sense of 'self'; mum and daughter have a right to decide how they want to be described and mum has a right not to take part in the ethnicity survey. The decision made by the class teacher results in lost opportunities – the opportunity to start a dialogue with mum, the opportunity to discuss the concept of self-identity with all the pupils in the class and the opportunity for the individual child to discuss her own situation in a supportive environment. The decision also ignores the fact that other children do not see the child as white and treat her differently.

Case study 3

Children in a nursery were painting self-portraits. A dual-heritage child was painting herself. The adult working with the group discussed each child's skin tone and took care to obtain paint of the nearest shade. There were lots of photographs of adults and children with various shades of skin colour on the wall near the painting area.

All the children in this group were able to identify themselves in terms of their physical appearance and skin colour and had positive images around to ensure that they all felt able to see themselves as part of wider groups within society. By discussing skin tone, the adult also created an opportunity for the children to discuss other issues, for example, why people call other people names because of their appearance, and what they could do if that happened.

Case study 4

A single white parent of two dual-heritage children has tried to ensure that the home reflects the two heritages. Language, clothes, food, art and music from both cultures are enjoyed by the family and there are close links with extended families on both sides. Despite their separation, parents have had honest, sometimes painful, discussions about the importance of and persistence needed in promoting the black heritage in a mainly white society, especially as the children reach teenage years and influences outside the home have greater impact. The parents are now exploring ways of encouraging the secondary school to look beyond the National Curriculum and league tables, and the family as a whole are investigating ways of tackling the lack of positive black images on television and in teenage magazines.

This case study illustrates the positive family experiences dual heritage children can have, and it is likely that these children will go on to become confident young people. The ability of the parents to overcome their own difficulties and move with the changes that are occurring for the children is important. The need to develop and maintain a two-way home–school dialogue is essential if the school is to meet individual needs and ensure that the children develop into confident young adults. The involvement of the whole family in looking at positive ways to address the issue of media images of black people will support the children in learning to deal in a positive way with any racism they encounter, as well as continuing to affirm their right to feel proud of who they are.

Factors affecting children's experiences

Many of the key issues that have been identified within our work as affecting the experiences of children of dual heritage can be broadly grouped within two areas, those relating to the child and family and those relating to the wider environment as illustrated in Figures 9.3 and 9.4.

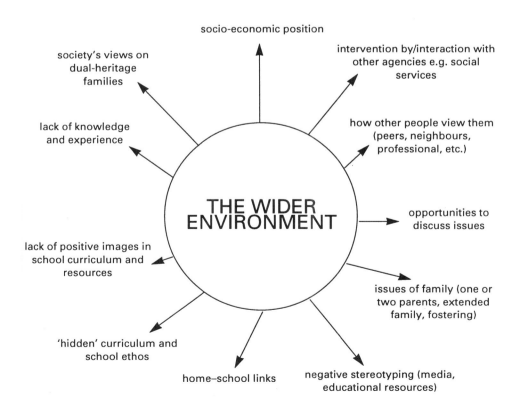

Figure 9.3 Issues that affect children's experiences and achievements(i)

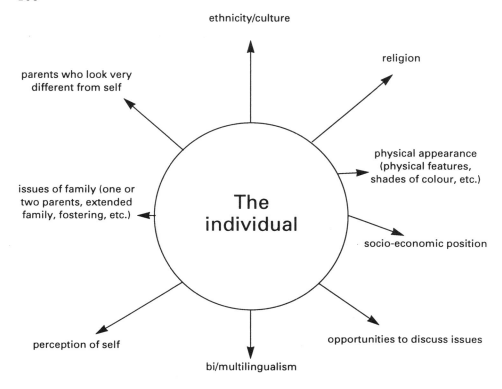

Figure 9.4 Issues that affect children's experiences and achievements (ii)

The perceptions held by other people of any particular family may vary from area to area, depending on the family itself, the local 'norm' and the fashionable attitudes within society at large. The interaction between the family and various agencies, including schools, may similarly vary from area to area, family to family, and will also be influenced by national policies and fashions. All of this, whether positive or negative, will have a bearing on any individual child's development.

The 'wider environment' includes not only a child's immediate physical and cultural environment but also attitudes and actions within the wider society, as these often interlink. For example, a child living in an inner-city, working-class, multicultural area is likely to have a vastly different experience to a child living in a rural, middle-class white area. The inner-city child may have a more positive experience in terms of having access to black culture, etc. but on the other hand may experience more prejudice within society at large as a black child within an inner city. The rural child may experience more isolation and lack immediate access to black culture but may be more 'acceptable' to society in general, conforming more to the acceptable white, middle-class norm even if s/he is black. The family's socio-economic position is important, as it is likely to influence not only a child's physical environment but also the value placed by her or his family on particular experiences.

Sometimes professionals faced with a child exhibiting inappropriate behaviour, may feel the child has an 'identity' problem due to his/her dual heritage and therefore fail to notice or acknowledge other factors of importance within that child's life. It is also important that professionals make sure that they do not determine a dual-heritage child's sense of self-identity purely by how black that professional considers them to be; not all black people like rice and peas or chicken tikka, so a dual-heritage child who does not choose them when they are offered does not necessarily have an 'identity problem'!

A recurring issue in our work, particularly when it involves parents, has been understanding the experiences of those parents themselves. Some white parents, in particular, may have found themselves in a situation where they feel that whatever they do they will be criticised and considered inadequate in terms of their ability to meet the needs of their child. The only apparent justification for this is the fact that they are not black. Some black parents need to understand and analyse their own experiences of racism in order to support their children. It is essential therefore to ensure that any work undertaken is done so with sensitivity to these issues. Our more successful workshops have been with one white and one black facilitator working together.

The school which a child attends will play a key role in his or her development. The ethnic mix within a particular school may not be as important as the levels of awareness of staff, the school ethos, and the relationship between home and school. If the school does not provide positive images of black and dual-heritage people, or the school curriculum focuses on a white world, it fails to meet the needs of its dual-heritage pupils. Where the relationship and communication between home and school are good, a child's needs are more likely to be met. For example, a dual-heritage child living in a predominantly white area may be experiencing racist abuse from other children inside or outside school. If the school is aware of this and has a supportive ethos there is plenty that they can do such as in terms of raising awareness and challenging racism as well as in supporting the development of a positive identity for the dual heritage child. If communication between the home and school is poor the school may not be aware of what is happening and therefore not see racism as an issue for that child.

The issues for each individual child are of course inextricably linked with their wider environment, but children living in similar environments may have very different experiences. The family's culture, religious influences, language, etc. will differ for each child and will be factors in development of his/her identity. A child's physical appearance will influence how he or she is perceived by others and who he or she identifies with. A not uncommon question from small children of dual heritage to their parent/s is 'When I grow up, will I look like you?' Family composition is also relevant; one child of dual heritage may be the only black member of the family, another may be part of predominantly black family. Therefore, whether or not children have opportunities to discuss these and other personal issues is also important in influencing understanding of themselves and other people.

It is important to ensure that issues to do with a child's heritage do not become confused with other emotional factors. For example, where one parent is caring for a child following the breakdown of a relationship they can in some cases, transfer their anger with the absent parent to the child. While this transference of anger can happen within any family, within a dual-heritage family the anger may be expressed in a racist way, or the child may perceive it as such. This could be very damaging, particularly if the absent parent is black, because the child may not have any positive images or support to counteract the message they receive. Therefore, the importance of separating the anger with a particular person, from anger with a group of people which includes the child, is clear. However, it is also important to note that a parent in this situation may be unaware of the impact of what they are doing and, with support, may well be able to separate their feelings about their adult relationship from their relationship with their child and, having done so, may then be able to meet their children's needs effectively.

Strategies for parents, carers and professionals

While the complexity of the issues involved is clear, it must be remembered at all times that being of dual heritage is not in itself a problem. It is the attitudes and behaviour of others that may make it so. However, the impact of these attitudes and behaviour on children can cause them difficulties in terms of self-image and self-esteem, which in turn can affect their whole lives. Many schools have started to recognise and address the needs of some minority ethnic children. They also need to take account of the specific experiences and needs of dual-heritage children and their families. In Coventry we have tried to facilitate this.

We have encouraged professionals to use and develop resources with positive images. We have discussed strategies for reflecting the cultural, linguistic and ethnic diversity in their nurseries, schools and in the wider society through the broad curriculum. We have explored ways of providing children with opportunities to discuss their own experiences and perceptions of self as part of personal and social education.

We have encouraged open and honest discussion between home and school, which is invaluable in supporting children. We have given parents/carers opportunities to raise issues with professionals, either by running joint workshops or by linking workshops so that suggestions made by parents have been brought to a later workshop for discussion by professionals. We have discussed with parents ways in which they contribute to their child's development, focusing on the duality of the child's heritage. We have discussed how gender, physical appearance, religion, language/dialect, food, clothes, music, books, family history, etc. contributed to the development of our own identity. For children of dual heritage it follows that, if they are to understand and feel comfortable with who they are, they need to have knowledge and experience of both sides of their heritage. By thinking about their children's experiences, parents are able to identify areas in which they feel they meet the child's needs and areas in which they may need assistance in the way of information or support. Also we have enabled parents to share with each other their experiences and strategies that they have used in particular situations, for example, raising an issue with a teacher or a family member or answering children's questions. When the black and white partners share parenting, the need to have an honest discussion of the issues concerning their children and their strategies for developing their children's self-esteem has been identified within our work as being of great importance.

The subject matter can be extremely emotional and we have found it important to allow time for people to talk about their own experiences before moving forward with the discussion on children's needs. Care needs to be taken however to ensure that 'off loading' does not take up too much time, as the sharing of experience is not the main aim of the discussion. We also give participants an opportunity to think about what they will do, in the short and longer term, to support the children with whom they live and/or work.

What next?

The work in Coventry is still developing. It is difficult to evaluate the success of what we are doing, but comments such as 'I had never thought about that before', or 'Now I know how to discuss it with the teachers', make us believe we have gone some way towards raising awareness. To the question 'What is the most useful thing you have learned?' the overwhelming response has been 'To be more positive about dual-heritage families', leading us to believe that we have gone some way towards changing attitudes. Many professionals have said they feel more confident about discussing the issues with their colleagues and parents. Many parents have welcomed the opportunities to share experiences and learn from one another – indicating that in the longer term, support groups for parents of dual-heritage children may be useful.

We have found many books and posters for young children with positive images of dual-heritage families. There is, however, a shortage of appropriate published materials, especially for older children, and we would like to work with others in the field of equal opportunities to raise publishers' and authors' awareness. In the meantime, many schools already have the best resource – their children, whose photographs can be used to produce their own materials.

Finally, while many parents, carers and professionals referred to the experiences recounted by their children, we want to facilitate ways for the children to have their own say about their experiences, their feelings and what action they would like to see.

10 Working with refugee children and their families

Jill Rutter

There are over 29,000 refugee children in British schools. They are a very diverse group of students and have wide-ranging psychosocial and educational needs, which may or may not be met. This chapter presents an educational framework for the support of refugee children, in particular examining ways in which refugee families can be encouraged to be involved in their child's education.

Who are refugees?

There are nearly 19 million asylum-seekers and refugees in today's world, more than at any other time in history. The migration of refugees is a growing challenge to governments, non-governmental organisations and international agencies – the number of refugees has doubled in a decade. In Britain many more schools now have refugees as students.

The word refugee is now part of everyday vocabulary. But it does have a precise legal[1] meaning. A person with refugee status is defined as someone who has fled from his or her home country, or is unable to return to it 'owing to a well-founded fear of being persecuted for reasons of race, religion, nationality, membership of a particular social group or political opinion' (1951 UN Convention). Asylum-seekers are people who have crossed an international border in search of safety (and refugee status) in another country. In Britain asylum-seekers are people who are waiting a Home Office decision as to whether they can remain.

Some 43,965 asylum-seekers and their dependents arrived in Britain in 1996. Their main countries of origin are listed in Table 10.1. Once an individual or family has arrived in Britain an immediate concern is to begin the process of applying for political asylum. An asylum application may be lodged at the port of entry, or at the Immigration and Nationality Department of the Home Office, after entry to Britain. On the basis of documentation given to the Immigration and Nationality Department, a decision is made. It can be one of three different outcomes: full refugees status, exceptional leave to remain (ELR) or a refusal of an asylum application. At present some 7 per cent of asylum-seekers are granted refugee status, 11 per cent ELR and 81 per cent are refused (Home Office 1996).

Table 10.1 Main countries of origin of refugee children in Britain

Country	Number of asylum-seekers 1995	Most usual home language
Colombia	525	Spanish
Poland	1,210	Polish, Romany[1]
Romania	770	Romanian, Romany, Hungarian
Turkey	1,820	Turkish and/or Kurdish (Kumanji)[2]
Former Yugoslavia	1,565	Bosnian (Serbo-Croat in Roman script), Albanian
Iran	615	Farsi[3]
Iraq	930	Arabic and/or Kurdish (Sorani)
Algeria	1,865	Arabic, French, Kabyle
Angola	555	Portuguese, sometimes Umbundu, Kimbundu, Kikongo
Ethiopia	585	Amharic, Oromo, Tigrinya
Ghana	1,915	English, Twi, Fante, Ewe, Ga
Kenya	1,395	English, Swahili, Kikuyu, Luo and others
Liberia	390	English, Krio, Kpelle
Nigeria	5,825	English, Yoruba, Ibo, Fulani, Hausa
Sierra Leone	855	Krio, English, Mende, Temme
Somalia	3,465	Somali, Brava, Arabic[4]
Sudan	345	Arabic, Dinka, Nuer and other southern languages, English
Tanzania	1,535	Swahili, English
Uganda	365	English, Luganda
Zaire	935	French, Lingala, Kikongo
Afghanistan	580	Dari, Pushtu[3]
China	790	Mandarin Chinese, Cantonese
India	3,255	Mostly Punjabi
Pakistan	2,915	Urdu, Pushlu
Sri Lanka	2,070	Tamil

[1] The majority of Polish asylum-seekers in 1995 were Romanys.
[2] In Turkey it has been forbidden to speak or publish in Kurdish until very recently. As a result very few families are literate in Kurdish.
[3] The Persian language is usually referred to as Farsi in Iran and Dari in Afghanistan.
[3] Many recent refugees from Somalia are from the Brava community who live in the southern coastal towns. They speak a dialect of Swahili called Brava.

The high proportion of those refused political asylum in Britain is a major cause for concern to human rights and refugee organisations. The latter is part of wide-ranging legislative and policy changes affecting the immigration and social rights of asylum-seekers in Britain. These changes are detailed in Table 10.2. In particular changes in social security policy and housing legislation may seriously affect the ability of refugee children to learn in schools. Those asylum-seekers who are entitled to income support are only entitled to 90 per cent of the personal allowances. But since 5 February 1996 the majority of new asylum-seekers have been deprived of any access to benefits. Since that date changes in social security regulations have denied two groups of asylum-seekers access to income support, housing benefit, free school meals, free prescriptions, uniform grants and further education courses at concessionary rates. All asylum-seekers who make their claims 'in-country' rather than at the port of entry are denied benefits; they amount to about 65 per cent of all asylum-seekers. Asylum-seekers who have been refused asylum now lose their benefits at the point of refusal rather than when the appeals process is exhausted.

Table 10.2 Main changes in asylum policy, 1984–1995

1984 Greater proportions of asylum-seekers are awarded ELR rather than refugee status.

1985 Visa requirements introduced for Sri Lankan nationals, making it more difficult for Tamils fleeing from northern Sri Linka to reach safety.

1986 Visa requirements introduced for Ghanaians.

1987 Immigration (Carriers' Liability) Act passed. This fines airlines and other carriers for transporting passengers, often potential asylum-seekers, who lack the correct travel documents. It makes airline employees surrogate immigration officers.

1987 Social security regulations change with asylum-seekers being reduced to 90 per cent of personal allowances.

1989 Visas introduced for Turkish nationals after Turkish Kurdish asylum-seekers arrive in Britain.

1990 Visas introduced for Ugandans. The Dublin Convention is signed between 12 EU countries.

1992 The Edinburgh Declaration on 'manifestly unfounded asylum applications'. Visas introduced for Bosnian nationals.

1993 The Asylum and Immigration (Appeals) Act and associated changes in immigration rules. This introduces a 'fast track' system at ports of entry, and restricts the right of asylum-seekers to be housed in permanent local authority accommodation. The proportions of asylum-seekers who are rejected increases from 16 per cent to 76 per cent.

1994 Visas for Sierra Leonean nationals.

1996 Social security regulations change, denying the majority of asylum-seekers access to income support, housing benefit, free school meals, low cost adult ESOL and other benefits. Those affected are asylum-seekers who apply 'in-country' and those appealing against refusal.

1996 The Asylum and Immigration Bill is debated. It proposes to list some countries of origin as safe and deny asylum-seekers from these countries access to the full asylum determination procedures. Aslylum-seekers may also be denied access to any form of local authority accommodation.

The Department for Social Security estimated that by the end of 1996 some 46,000 asylum-seekers will no longer have access to benefits (Refugee Council and Save the Children Fund 1996). Among this group will be many children, for whom local authority social service departments will be forced to make provision under the Children Act 1990. At the time of writing some children of asylum-seekers without benefits have been judged to be 'in need' by social services departments and are being supported by Children Act Section 17 funding. These families have been allocated temporary housing and a subsistence allowance that is less than income support.

Other families may have slipped through support networks. Refugee and asylum-seeking families are also taking in friends and family who have been affected by the benefit changes, stretching scarce resources still further (Refugee Council and the Save the Children Fund 1996). Loss of benefits and the threat of loss of benefits are likely to cause asylum-seeking families great stress. Such anxieties can be picked up by the youngest member of a family.

The Asylum and Immigration (Appeals) Act 1993 restricted asylum-seekers rights to social housing in Britain. If asylum-seekers are to be housed by local authorities or housing associations under vulnerability clauses in the 1985 Housing Act, that family may not be housed in permanent local authority accommodation as long as they are asylum-seekers. The 1996 Asylum Bill, being debated in parliament at the time of writing introduces further restrictions on asylum-seekers rights to social housing. It is likely that all asylum-seekers will lose their rights to social housing and may be entirely dependent on the private sector. (The proportions of all school children in temporary accommodation is likely to increase if the present Housing Bill becomes law.)

The result of the changes to housing legislation is a greater geographic mobility among children who are asylum-seekers. Unpublished doctoral research in two schools in areas where there is a great deal of temporary accommodation indicates that the move on rate for refugee children in these schools is between 70 and 100 per cent in one academic year. The implications for the child and school are enormous (Shelter 1995).

Refugee children in Britain

Using local authority language surveys the Refugee Council estimates that there are approximately 29,000 newly arrived refugee children in British schools, the majority of whom – 89 per cent – are attending schools in Greater London. Some refugee groups are present in reasonably large numbers within a particular local authority. Other refugee communities are widely dispersed, across Greater London or a wider area.

Young refugees are a diverse group of students, who have a wide range of educational and social needs. They may:

- have suffered overwhelming trauma in their home countries;
- have suffered an enormous drop in their standard of living and other major changes;
- be living with families who do not know their educational and social rights;
- have had an interrupted education in their countries of origin;
- not be cared for by their parents or usual carers;
- be living in temporary accommodation in Britain, and have attended many schools in the UK;
- speak little or no English on arrival in Britain;
- suffer bullying or isolation on arrival in school;
- have no rights to study in the further education sector.

With these needs in mind, refugee children need flexible forms of support which encompass:

- school induction practices, designed to welcome children who have recently come from abroad and are usually admitted during the term;
- English language support;
- help in maintaining the first language;
- appropriate psychological intervention for those refugee children who need it;
- programmes to counter hostility to refugees in schools and to raise awareness about refugees;
- in-service training for teachers;
- home–school liaison with parents who may speak little English and have little understanding of how the British education system works;
- local authority housing policies which provide refugee children with the maximum amount of stability.

The availability of specialist support to meet the needs of refugee children varies across Britain. Refugee children with language needs are usually given English language support by local authority and school staff funded by Section 11 of the 1966 Local Government Act. The quantity and quality of language support varies, and there are three areas where improvements are needed.

Firstly, for many English language staff working with refugee children and most refugee communities is a new experience. Staff may lack knowledge about the backgrounds of refugee children, and the particular social conditions which impact on their ability to learn. Secondly, some groups of refugee children may have missed large parts of their prior education. Children may be attending primary and secondary schools in Britain, having never attended school before, and lacking literacy in their first language. There is much room for improvement in the way that these children are given support. Lastly, there is a need to improve communicate with parents as to how language support is delivered.

Some 11 LEAs presently have Section 11 funded projects working specifically or mainly with refugee children and young people. (Another LEA has

a school-based education project funded by the Single Regeneration Budget.) One such project, based in the London Borough of Enfield employs
eight staff. A team of 'refugee support teachers' are providing English language and other forms of support for newly arrived refugee children. The
teachers also deliver in-service training and help schools develop positive
practices. The project employs the part-time services of an educational psy-
chologist and an educational social worker.

Section 210 of the 1988 Education Reform Act has also been used to fund
education projects working with refugee children and adults. It is a fund
that pays 50 per cent of an LEA's costs for projects that work with children
and adults in LEAs where there are reception centres. That it is limited to
LEAs where there are reception centres means that few LEAs are able to
apply for Section 210 funding. At present some seven local education
authorities are in receipt of funding for such work.

Several voluntary organisations are working with refugee children.
The Refugee Council supports unaccompanied refugee children. It runs
two children's homes and has a panel of advisers for unaccompanied
refugee children. It also works in schools and colleges, providing
advice, teacher training and specialist publications for teachers and students. The Medical Foundation for the Care of Victims of Torture employs
a child psychotherapist working with refugee children. She also provides
in-service training for teachers. Nafsiyat, an intercultural counselling
project is offers one-to-one psychotherapeutic counselling to young
refugees, runs group counselling in some schools and colleges and is
training members of refugee communities so that they can provide
counselling themselves. Barnados are working with children and families
in temporary accommodation. Some refugee community groups are
working with children, particularly in the provision of supplementary
schools.

Home–school liaison with refugee children

In recent years much has been made of parental choice and parental
involvement in education. But for many refugee parents this has been
rhetoric; they have very poor links with their child's school and little
involvement in their child's education. It is worth reflecting on why this is
so.

Past experiences may make some refugee parents fearful of authorities,
including schools. Current legislation and statements that public services
may have to check the immigration status of users may have added to a climate of suspicion in Britain (Hansard 14.7.95). The fear that a school may
'report' a parent to immigration authorities is real for some refugee parents.
The uncertain position asylum-seeking parents find themselves in may
make them nervous of challenging institutions.

Refugees have come from countries where the education system is different to Britain. The age of entry to formal education may be higher and students' progression routes different. Teaching may be more formal and teacher centred. Schools may be less well-equipped and children have little experience of things such as laboratory practicals. As a consequence parents who are newly arrived in Britain may be unfamiliar with how the education system works and what is expected of them. Misunderstandings arise, particularly regarding a child's progression by age through the education system (rather than progression by passing and examination at the end of the school year). Refugee parents may also expect their children to receive formal teaching in English. Language is another factor preventing parental participation in education; about 70 per cent of asylum-seekers arrive in Britain speaking little or no English (Carey-Wood 1995).

If schools are to achieve positive links with refugee parents, the overall ethos of the school is important. Schools should make parents feel that families from different linguistic and cultural backgrounds are valued and that the school is part of the community it serves. A school should be welcoming and parents made to feel that they can always enter and talk to staff. First impressions are important!

Parents who speak little or no English will need an interpreter and for written information to be translated if they are to make an effective contribution to their child's education. Although it may be relatively easy to arrange the translation of standard letters, other forms of translation and interpreting may be more difficult to arrange. Family members do sometimes interpret, but this is not always possible or indeed and ideal arrangement. A trained interpreter – essential at a child's admission interview – costs money. Many local authorities charge schools £16–20 per hour. At a time when finances are constrained, this is expenditure some schools are unwilling to meet. In some local authorities the population of some refugee groups is very small, and no local authority interpreting services exist. In the 32 London local authorities some seventeen provide Somali interpreters, nine provide French-speaking interpreters, thirteen provide Arabic interpreters and twelve provide Turkish-speaking interpreters. Very few London local authorities cater for languages such as Serbo-Croat or Amharic (Refugee Council 1994).

Other issues can arise where interpreters are used. Many refugee and immigrant communities are divided along political lines. For example the Turkish-speaking community includes Turkish Cypriots, Turkish Kurds and ethnic Turks from Turkey. Organised within this linguistic group are many different political parties, from far-right Turkish nationalist groups to far-left groups. Interpreters can be associated with these groups, and may not be trusted by the family for whom they are interpreting. In one London borough, interpreters from the Turkish embassy were used in schools to interpret for Kurdish families who had fled the persecution of the Turkish state.

Using interpreters is a complex issue. Below are some practical guidelines for interviewing a family through an interpreter:

- check that the interpreter and the family speak the same language or dialect;
- allow time for a pre-interview briefing with the interpreter to talk about the content of the interview and technical terms that may be used;
- check that the family is happy with the interpreter;
- ask the interviewer to explain to the family that the interview is confidential;
- allow enough time for the interview – it will take a longer period of time where interpreters are used;
- at the end of the interview check that the family have understood everything or want to ask any more questions;
- spend a short period of time at the end of the interview to debrief the interpreter.

It is important to evaluate schools' induction practice. In some local authorities families have to attend several interviews with LEA staff and the school before a child is admitted. This may present practical difficulties. Staff that conduct these interviews may not always be aware and sensitive to refugees' past experiences and current needs. Schools should try and show parents round the school and talk about differences in learning methods and the curriculum between Britain and a child's home country.

Several LEAs and voluntary organisations are involved in programmes to achieve positive home–school links. The London Boroughs of Camden, Merton and Croydon are employing bilingual staff from refugee communities to work as home–school liaison teachers. The London Borough of Haringey has a Section 11 funded project to encourage parental involvement in education. A team of 'parental involvement workers' from different minority communities, including the Somali and Turkish Kurdish community are attached to the education department. They work in schools helping teachers with admissions interviews and assessments, and where particular problems arise. The staff also run 'parental involvement workshops' where refugee parents are guided through the education system, how they can help their child's education and what to do when problems arise. The parental involvement workers also contact children and families via community groups.

The London Language and Literacy Unit is funded to work with refugee children and their families. It has targeted the Somali community, after a disproportionate number of Somali boys were excluded from some schools. As well as working with individual Somali students and their families, to facilitate their reintegration into school, the London Language and Literacy Unit has produced a booklet and conducted workshops that aim to encourage parents to help their child with reading (London Language and Literacy Unit 1994). Individual schools have organised 'new in the area parents coffee mornings' or meetings with particular groups of refugee parents.

Conclusions

There are some excellent initiatives to improve home–school liaison among refugee communities. The approaches taken and the lessons learnt on these projects need to be disseminated. The following recommendations are made as a conclusion:

- Local education authorities and schools must be encouraged to develop positive policy and practice towards asylum-seekers and refugees that includes the development of positive home–school links.
- Section 11 funding for home–school liaison projects must continue. Section 11 funding must provide long-term support and not be allocated as short-term grants.
- A welcoming school is the type of school that will achieve positive home–school links. Induction practice is a key to this. Schools must evaluate what happens to children who are admitted mid-term to a new school.
- Admissions staff should receive some training about refugees' needs and on the use of interpreters.
- Refugee parents need to be given written information on how the British education system works and also be given the opportunity to raise questions and concerns about their child's schooling.

Notes

1. The legal definition of who is a refugee is taken from the 1951 UN Convention and 1967 Protocol Relating to the Status of Refugees. These two legal instruments enshrine the rights of asylum-seekers and refugees, preventing them being returned to countries where they fear persecution. The UK has acceded to the 1951 UN Convention and 1967 Protocol.

References

Ahearn, F. and Athey, J. (1991) *Refugee Children: theory, research and services.* Harvard, USA: Harvard University Press.

Carey-Wood, J. (1995) *The Settlement of Refugees in Britain*. Home Office Studies No. 41. London: HMSO/Home Office Research and Planning Unit.

Daycare Trust (1995) *Reaching First Base: meeting the needs of refugee children from the Horn of Africa*. London: Daycare Trust.

Finlay, R. and Reynolds, J. (1987) *Social Work and Refugees*. Cambridge: National Extension College.

Further Education Unit (1994) *Refugee Education and Training*. London: FEU.

Harvard Programme in Refugee Trauma (1992) *Repatriation and Disability: a community study of health, mental health and social functioning of Khmer residents at Site Two*. Volume Two: Khmer Children. Harvard: Harvard Programme in Refugee Trauma.

Home Office (1996) *Asylum Statistics 1995: Statistical Update*. London: Home Office Statistical Division.

Klein, G. (1993) *Education Towards Race Equality*. London: Cassell.

London Language and Literacy Unit (1994) *Teaching Your Child to Read*. London: Language and Literacy Unit.

McCallin M (Ed.) (1982) *The Psychological Well-Being of Refugee Children*. Geneva: International Catholic Child Bureau.

Maksoud, M. (1992) 'Assessing War Trauma in Children: a case study of Lebanese children', *Journal of Refugee Studies*, 5, 1. Oxford: OUP.

Melzak, S. and Warner, R. (1992) *Integrating Refugee Children into Schools*. London: Medical Foundation and Minority Rights Group.

Office For Standards in Education (1994) *Educational Support for Minority Ethnic Communities*. London: OFSTED.

Refugee Council (1994) *Helping Refugee Children in Schools*. London: Refugee Council.

Refugee Council and the Save the Children Fund (1996) *No Refugee for Children: the impact on children of withdrawing benefits and housing from asylum seekers*. London: Refugee Council/SCF.

Ressler, E., Boothby, N. and Steinbock, D. (1988) *Unaccompanied Children*. Oxford: Oxford University Press.

Richman, N. (1993) *Communicating with Children: helping children in distress*. London: Save the Children Fund.

Rutter, J. (1994) *Refugee Children in the Classroom*. Stoke-on-Trent: Trentham Books.

Rutter, M. (1990) 'Resilience in the Face of Adversity: protective factors and resistance to psychiatric disorder', *British Journal of Psychiatry*, 147, pp. 598–611.

Save the Children Fund (1994) *The Somali Community in Cardiff*. Wales: Save the Children Fund.

Shelter (1995) *No Place to Learn: homelessness and education*. London: Shelter.

United Nations High Commissioner for Refugees (1994) *Refugee Children: guidelines on protection and care*. Geneva: UNHCR.

Warner, R. (1991a) *Voices from Eritrea*. London: Minority Rights Group.

Warner, R. (1991b) *Voices from Kurdistan*. London: Minority Rights Group.

Warner, R. (1991c) *Voices from Somalia*. London: Minority Rights Group.

Warner, R. (1995a) *Voices from Angola*. London: Minority Rights Group.

Warner, R. (1995b) *Voices from Zaire*. London: Minority Rights Group.

11 'Auntie – ji, please come and join us, just for an hour.' The role of the bilingual education assistant in working with parents with little confidence

Sheila Karran

Introduction

This chapter considers strategies which aim to inform parents about their child's learning, particularly in those situations where that learning is accredited by means of the completion of parent courses. The chapter focuses upon the question of how we involve those parents who are reluctant to take part in the courses offered for linguistic and cultural aspects. It will make reference to the importance of having staff or access to personnel with whom parents can comfortably identify and communicate.

It is generally agreed that an individual's attitudes about education are founded on that person's own experiences of 'formal learning'. These experiences vary greatly when considering differences within class and culture. However, it is dangerous to make general assumptions from surveys of individual groups and this chapter carries such a health warning.

The definition here of 'courses' for parents includes any information exchange within the range of a structured dialogue taking place between teachers and parents on a regular basis and that where parents gain some national accreditation for their learning.

Courses for parents in Coventry since the 1970s

In some cultures the role of the educators is seen as distinct and separate from the role of parenting, and educators may need to take some time explaining and illustrating how the child can benefit from partnership and continuity of educational experience across early years settings and home (Siraj-Blatchford 1994).

For the past two decades home–school work in Coventry has been committed to parental involvement and parental empowerment. This has been demonstrated by reading workshops; the family curriculum; the 'Put Your-

self in Their Place' series of participatory activities to extend parents' understanding of children's learning; the home early learning programme; home
school link worker parent courses which enable parents to encourage other
parents to be involved in school activities. In 1980 the 'Eburne – Further
Education College Outreach Programme' enabled hundreds of inner-city
parents to take up, each year, 'free' GCSE and A level classes. A course
about working with young children and their families was accredited with
the RSA in 1984. The consequence of this has been that dozens of mothers
have since become employed as valued education assistants by Coventry
schools. Several have gone on to higher education and are now in teaching
or social work. Today Coventry has over ten courses accredited with the
Open College Network that specifically focus on the involvement of parents in their child's education.

Throughout the 1970s and 1980s Coventry was renowned for its vast
production of home-grown community education certificates which
acknowledged completion of a course. Successful parents were able to
present these at interviews. In 1996 these have been mostly replaced by
Open College Network and the NVQ Child Care and Education Level 11
portfolios.

Support for bilingual pupils and their families

Coventry LEA has also been committed for almost two decades to English
language support for its bilingual pupils. About 6000 such children are supported each year by a team of 150 full-time and part-time teachers and 60
full-time and part-time bilingual education assistants. The latter are almost
all placed in the early years settings in schools where the need for language
support is identified, using here a bilingual approach to enhance the child's
learning opportunities.

> Language makes accessible culture, culture includes the bilingual pupils' experi-
> ence, and experience shapes knowledge ... If teaching strategies encourage,
> value and support the use of bilingual pupils' home language, the children are
> more likely to share their language and culture freely without feeling that they
> are the centre of attention.
>
> (Blackledge 1994)

This applies equally to their bilingual parents.

The role of bilingual assistants in courses for parents

Part of the bilingual education assistant's role is to take opportunities to
share the child's learning progress with the parent. To gather parents
together in a group for this purpose is cost-effective in respect of staff and
it is mutually supportive for the parents.

Many of the bilingual education assistants have completed an OCN course about how to facilitate learning opportunities within parent groups. They usually begin by co-tutoring on parent courses with a home–school links teacher. After which they go on to work with an experienced parent working with new parent groups.

Why do parents embark upon accredited courses which so often demand vast amounts of their time and energy? Generally, the intention is to gain qualifications and experience that may lead them to paid work with children. Also more and more committed parents, particularly mothers, have been encouraged to take their first step into the realm of further education. Parents who have attended courses often say they have developed a greater insight in their own child's learning; they are better equipped to support this learning; and above all they have achieved greater confidence in their own ability.

Mirpuri- and Sylheti-speaking families

As this new-found confidence is a positive factor for so many parents we need to focus on some who are least likely to benefit by courses for parents. This chapter focuses on the experiences of Mirpuri and Bangladeshi families for the reason that these two groups share certain social and educational concerns. The greatest concern is that Coventry children from these two communities make up the largest number of pupils, proportionally, requiring additional English language support. Teachers fear that these children are failing to gain access to the whole curriculum. This is a particular worry when the children are still at this basic level of English in Year One and in some cases, subsequent years. The Sylheti dialect, being similar to the Bangla language, is used by most of the Bangladeshi families in Coventry. The Mirpuri dialect although similar to Panjabi (Urdu) is used by a small minority of Asian families in Coventry. Both of these dialects are spoken and not written. When information is translated for the Mirpuri and Sylheti community it is written in Urdu script and Bangla respectively. A similar example in Britain might be in the northeast of England where the Geordie dialect speaking families would get standard English written letters sent from school. This doesn't present much of a difficulty for such parents where they are used to seeing written standard English and hearing it spoken on the radio and television. However, this is not generally the case for the Mirpuri- and Sylheti-speaking families who, brought up in Mirpur and Bangladesh, will probably not have had as much exposure to the media.

Within the Asian community, when both parents of preschool children are out at work the children are often cared for by grandparents. Many of these children are starting school with a limited range of vocabulary in their first language and almost no experience of hearing and speaking English. For Mirpuri and Bangladeshi children from relatively small Asian communities in Coventry their linguistic isolation is accentuated.

The faith shared by the majority of Mirpuri and Bangladeshi families is that of Islam. According to Sitara Khan (1985), many Moslem families share a similar attitude towards British education and racism in Britain. She states:

> Muslim parents feel that the British educational system has failed them and their children. In general Muslim children have consistently failed to fulfil themselves academically within the system and have often emerged at the end of it feeling estranged from their parents and their culture.

Mirpuri- and Sylheti-speaking pupils are sometimes overlooked because they are the smallest minority ethnic group within the school. Unless there is someone available who speaks the Sylheti language and Mirpuri dialect, the language and dialect used by these pupils can remain unidentified for some considerable time by the school.

During the autumn term 1995 four Mirpuri and Sylheti bilingual assistants and two case work officers from the home–school links team talked to some of the mothers about their own personal experiences of education in Kashmir and Bangladesh. They were particularly interested in talking with the mothers as they found that it was the mothers who generally underestimated their role in their child's education. Some of the comments are given in Table 11.1.

A few weeks later the same home–school links staff conducted a small survey by listening to 30 Sylheti and 20 Mirpuri-speaking mothers talking about their involvement in their own child's school – see Table 11.2.

Involvement of Sylheti- and Mirpuri-speaking parents in courses in three primary schools

The first school

The first school is an urban primary school with over 500 children on role of which 5 per cent of children are from Sylheti-speaking families. Over the years the school had been successful in running several Open College Network courses for parents. Some of the courses were open to all parents. Other courses were geared to attract parents from specific ethnic groups so that in one instance the Gujerati bilingual education assistant was made available to recruit and support Gujerati mothers who were anxious about their competency in the use of English. The African-Caribbean education assistant and the deputy headteacher together offered a course for the African-Caribbean parents and parents of dual-heritage children. Usually the recruitment for courses about the curriculum would focus on parents whose children attended a particular year group.

In October 1994 the school offered a course for Sylheti-speaking parents with children in the nursery and reception class. The course was delivered by an English teacher and a Sylheti-speaking bilingual education assistant.

Table 11.1 Mothers' comments

My memories of school in Bangladesh/Mirpur	What I think is most different about schools in Britain
'If we didn't do well enough we were made to do that year over again.'	'In the primary school the children just seem to play.'
'My father refused to pay for my education after my ninth birthday as the teacher said I was a slow learner.'	'They are not given enough homework.'
'I learnt the ABC and the numbers 1 – 100 at five years old. I didn't understand what it meant though.'	'The British teachers' life must be easy because they are just child minding, they are not teaching.'
'We were taught that it was impolite to have eye contact with our elders or those in authority.'	'I think they learn things more slowly in Britain but they do understand what they are learning.'
'The quick learners at school were given responsibility to teach the slow learners. Those who had difficulty learning were punished with the stick, with a detention or writing lines.'	'The children here are encouraged to question the teachers. We could never do that.'
	'Here children aren't afraid when they are learning in school. They seem to enjoy it. I think it's better.'

Table 11.2 Home–school links survey

Are there any reasons which prevent you from coming into your children's school? (Please tick)

	SYLHETI- SPEAKING MOTHERS%	MIRPURI- SPEAKING MOTHERS
a) I work during the day	3	18
b) I have too much work to do in the home	53	55
c) I have a younger child/ren not yet at school	20	36
d) I speak very little English	27	73
e) Other members of my family speak English and talk to the teachers instead of me	3	91

That is to say that the initial content was delivered in English and translated with further explanations in Sylheti. Discussion took place in Sylheti and translated back into English. The course was called 'Parents and Learning' and aimed at explaining the components of a successful school. Of the seven mothers who began the course, one had a rudimentary understanding of English, the others spoke and understood very little English. None of them had any formal education. Their children's illnesses prevented three of them from attending every session. There were ten sessions in all. The final session focused on evaluating the course. The headteacher joined in for this and presented course attendance certificates.

The general consensus from the mothers was that they had enjoyed the course and were genuinely sorry that they had missed certain sessions. The mothers had completed most of the science, language and maths activities with their children at home. They were asked what their greatest fear had been when they embarked on the course. They said it was the fear of making a fool of themselves and being shown up by not being able to read and write Bangla as well as the English language. They said that they felt safer with a group of Sylheti speakers only. They were asked how the course could have been improved. The one who understood a little English said that she would have liked more practice writing English. The others said they would like to have started to learn English at the same time as learning about the school. They asked for the next course to be about disciplining children. One said and others agreed with her: 'My greatest fear is that my child will no longer respect me when my child's English becomes much better than mine'.

Summary of the school's strategy

The positive outcomes were that:

- the parents felt more confident learning alongside others with whom they closely identified;
- they were able to discuss complex issues in Sylheti that wouldn't have been possible in English.

On the negative side:

- there was pressure from their families for the women to concentrate their energies on learning English.

It is therefore recommended that courses should:

- combine learning English with learning about children;
- attempt to enable different Asian language groups to learn together so that the most isolated groups build confidence in mixing with others;
- encourage discussions to go on within separate language groups and English to be the main language used for delivery and recording key words and phrases.

As a result, materials have been prepared for the next course on 'Handling Children's Behaviour' within the context of learning to read and write English. In fact the next course was later delivered as one of the twice-weekly English classes and included other Asian parents learning English. The Asian languages represented within the group of fifteen mothers were Malay, Gujerati, Urdu, Panjabi as well as Sylheti. All the mothers completed the course achieving OCN accreditation at Entry Level.

The second school

This school is another large urban primary school and has almost equal numbers of families who are English, Gujerati, Panjabi and fewer Mirpuri speakers. The staff were concerned that, although the majority of Mirpuri-speaking mothers would come to school to bring their children and some would attend their children's medical examinations, they were reluctant to discuss with the teacher their children's educational progress. The staff had always known that this was probably caused by the mothers' lack of confidence in their spoken English. The staff also found that the Mirpuri-speaking mothers were reticent to join the English class for adults and were also reticent to come into the nursery family sessions. The appointment of a Mirpuri-speaking bilingual education assistant certainly improved the communication between the staff and the parents. However, the early years staff particularly wanted to explain just how much parents can support their children's learning. A parental involvement programme was planned to operate from the second half of the spring term and to start with the nursery. By this stage in the academic year the nursery children had settled in to the routine and were less likely to be upset by any changes, however slight.

The school is now fortunate to have bilingual staff, or access to staff who can communicate with parents from each of the four main language groups. The Mirpuri-speaking mothers understandably tended to cluster together when bringing and collecting their children and they were by now comfortable conversing with the Mirpuri bilingual education assistant on a daily basis. An invitation to come into the nursery one afternoon a week for three successive weeks was offered to the Mirpuri-speaking mothers. During the afternoon sessions different activities were taking place where parents and children were encouraged to interact. The staff explained the educational value of the activities and how similar learning experiences could be tried out at home. The bilingual education assistant explained how she sold the idea to the parents. The dialogue tended to go as follows: 'Auntie-ji, please come in to the nursery next Wednesday afternoon, just for an hour. We're doing some cooking with the children and could do with your help. You can bring a friend'.

Initially, she said that there were protests from the mothers about too much work to do at home or having younger children who could not be left. However, after it was explained that the mothers would get a chance to see how their nursery children were progressing, they agreed. Most parents attended the three sessions. The nursery staff were pleased to answer their questions, such as, 'Is — mixing with the other children?', 'Does she talk in English or our language when she's here?', 'Does he do what he's told?'

The mothers were encouraged to take part in the activities. Where they preferred just to observe, this preference was respected. Although the school particularly targeted the mothers of the nursery children, fathers and grandparents and other relatives were also welcomed. The nursery staff invited parents from the English, Gujerati and Panjabi families in turn to attend similar nursery sessions.

Summary of the school's strategy

The positive outcomes were:
- the daily exchanges with the parents were now shared by all the staff and not only the bilingual assistant;
- the children's attitude towards their work changed. They took a more serious, interested approach, as though they were thinking, 'It's OK now that my mum approves of this';
- the mothers began to talk about the educational activities that they had been doing with their children at home.

On the negative side:
- the Mirpuri mothers didn't progress to becoming part of the parent and toddler group as did the other more confident groups.

Recommendations:
- take into consideration the timing of Ramadan in the year as this inevitably curtails the involvement of Muslim parents;

- greater explanation and encouragement needs to be given to the Mirpuri mothers regarding the benefits for pre-nursery children by attending the parent and toddler session.

The third school

Here the nursery class has a family session every Wednesday morning. Eighty per cent of their children are from families of Bangladeshi, Pakistani or Gujerati heritage. The majority faith is Islam. This urban primary school nursery class is particularly successful in its family session attendance. The Sylheti-speaking mothers, who had previously been reticent in attending, were encouraged by the presence of the newly appointed Sylheti-speaking bilingual education assistant in 1992. The family session is truly a family session. Some times as many as 30 parents, aunts, uncles, grandparents plus their preschool children come into the nursery. The nursery children are only allowed to attend if they are accompanied by an adult carer. Other younger siblings are also welcomed. Every week an activity for the adults is offered. The activities alternate from being adult centred to being child centred. For example, one Wednesday family session offers jewellery making. The next session might be about the educational value of children using paint to express their ideas, followed by sharing and cooking different traditional recipes.

The secret of the success in this family session is that no visiting adult is put under pressure. The monolingual staff concentrate upon engaging the children in stimulating activities; the bilingual staff focus on the parents/carers. The latter may be in the activity corner or move between the other adults who may wish to sit and observe or chat in small groups with others who share the same home language. Some adults stay for as little as half an hour; some stay all morning. No one is ever made to feel that they must become involved in any activity which makes them feel uncomfortable. However, increasingly parents/carers do become more involved. Some parents have offered to share their own particular skills with others. At present the 'activity' corner is embarking upon an Open College Network ten-session craft course. The Sylheti parents are assured of moral support from the Sylheti bilingual education assistant should they feel they would like to take part.

Summary of school's strategy

The positive outcomes are that:
- the parents/carers feel confident to attend on their own terms. Within this non-threatening atmosphere adults are more likely to try out initiatives new to them;
- the more confident parents began to take the initiative to provide or suggest a tutor for the week's activity.

This cross-cultural skill-exchange continues to thrive.

On the negative side:

- the morning session is labour-intensive i.e. staff to look after the children (mostly pre-nursery age), bi-lingual staff to communicate with the parents/carers;
- the minority European white parents now rarely attend the morning family session as they feel marginalised.

Recommendations:

- to ensure staff make maximum effort to encourage families from all ethnic groups to attend;
- to capitalise on offers of extra staff such as work experience students to attend the family session to share some of the responsibility.

Conclusion

For parents to participate in the daily life of an early years' setting there must be real and obvious commitment from staff. It is not enough to use the rhetoric of parents as 'partners' in the education of their children. Some educators do use such phrases, and through using these words feel committed to them. In reality this is not always the case, and it is all too easy to neglect the most vulnerable and needy parents (Siraj-Blatchford 1994).

This chapter has emphasised the crucial role of a bilingual member of staff. Without doubt, this is the one of most effective factors in the involvement of minority ethnic families who are not confident in their use of English and their acceptance in an unfamiliar environment. The ideal is, of course, to employ appropriate qualified teachers who are themselves from minority ethnic families. School budgets rarely enable immediate employment of bilingual staff to accommodate all the languages that the school requires. In this situation a helpful suggestion might be to cultivate and enlist the support of the most confident of the minority ethnic parents as volunteer home school link workers to encourage other parents (Karran 1985).

As well as employing bilingual staff, the school and nursery staff need to ensure that they consider the hidden messages that their classroom environment and practices transmit to the community that they serve.

> An atmosphere should be created where ethnic minority parents feel comfortable to come and interact with children and their educators. Home–school links are vital to this endeavour and can be promoted in a number of ways. Parents should have access to information about their child. Letters should be translated and efforts made to use interpreters with parents who are still learning English. Bilingual signs should be displayed around the classroom and outside it. Dual-language books and tapes should be displayed where they are easily accessible. Use can be made of a variety of multicultural resources offering positive images through such things as poster, play utensils, dolls, games, puzzles and music tapes. The curriculum on offer should also incorporate a variety of festivals, family life and art and craft materials. If the classroom resources and curriculum

reflect the children's lives, the children are more likely to want to engage in and learn from the activities we provide.

(Siraj-Blatchford 1994)

I would add that as this affects the learning process of minority ethnic children it also affects that of their parents.

If the Bangladeshi and Mirpuri communities are feeling isolated within Coventry's inner city, where there is a relatively high 19 per cent of Asian pupils in school, then account must be taken of the effect of isolation of the geographically scattered Asian families in the Coventry surburban schools. All the recommendations mentioned here have relevance for home–school liaison with minority ethnic groups generally.

Finally, courses which involve parents in the process of their children's learning have proved to be an ideal opportunity to create a teacher, parent and child partnership. Courses offer the school, and its parent groups of mixed ethnicity, the benefits of a rich intercultural and educational exchange. Parents and teachers are able to discuss issues, consider each others' concerns and bring about appropriately supportive changes both at school and in the home.

Summary of strategies which encourage the involvement of isolated groups of Asian parents in their child's learning

- Consider resources which acknowledge cultural heritage and language;
- outwardly value parents' skills as well as the skills of being a parent;
- provide access to an adult worker or volunteer who can share the same cultural identity and home language;
- offer activities, discussions and courses which address the important issue of children's education;
- offer opportunities to parents for improving their English literacy and oracy skills;
- offer parents practical activities to use at home with their child which complement the child's learning in class. (e.g. IMPACT maths). Check first on the cultural acceptability of the activity from an informed source;
- listen to concerns parents may have;
- be prepared to act upon suggestions made by parents.

References

Blackledge, A. (1994) *Teaching Bilingual Children* (p 58). Stoke-on-Trent: Trentham Books.

Karran, S. (1985) 'Volunteer Parent Home School Link Workers', *Outlines*, 2, p.41, CEDC.

Khan, S. (1985) *The Education of Muslim Girls*, p.33. Leeds: Leeds Community Education Council.

Siraj-Blatchford, I. (1994) *The Early Years: laying the foundations for the racial equality*, pp.51, 94, 95. Stoke-on-Trent: Trentham Books.

12 The contribution of parent groups to home– school links in Cambridgeshire

Alison Shilela (co-ordinator) with Christine Corkhill, Susie Hall, Doreen Medcraft, Bethan Rees, Mehbubar Rehman and Naseer Sethi

The context

At the start of the current Section 11 project in 1992, the Cambridgeshire Multicultural Education Service identified as one of its targets the increased participation of minority ethnic parents in the education system throughout the county. This need had been identified locally through consultation with community groups and needs analyses carried out by Section 11 staff. The research showed that gaining access to schools can be difficult for parents whose first language is not English, especially if they come from a different cultural background.

While home–school liaison is an integral part of the work of the Cambridgeshire Multicultural Education Service and is fulfilled in various ways, this chapter will consider formalised parents groups as a way of strengthening the partnership between home and school.

Cambridgeshire is a large county with a diverse profile. In the north of the county, communities from minority ethnic groups, e.g. Pakistani, African-Caribbean, Chinese, are well established, mainly in Peterborough, whereas the backdrop in the south is very different. Cambridge city comprises communities who are very mobile, in part due to the fact that people move to Cambridge because of university links, e.g. visiting lecturers and their families, as well as established communities, such as the Bangladeshi community and the African-Caribbean community.

This chapter describes four projects set up in Cambridgeshire through working partnerships between the multicultural education service, local schools, community groups and community education. While each project differs in its approach, all four have common aims and similar outcomes. The projects described have been developed at different times and by different people over a three-year period.

The aims of the projects

The aims of the four initiatives can be described as follows:

- to help parents from minority ethnic groups to participate in their children's education through familiarising them with the educational system, thus raising the achievement of black and bilingual children;
- to develop, strengthen, and maintain good relationships between black and bilingual parents, pupils and schools;
- to facilitate a local support group for black and bilingual parents offering information, advice and skills identified by the parents themselves, e.g. literacy and oracy in English;
- to establish a forum for discussion;
- to encourage parents to become involved with the management of schools by organising training for prospective parent governors.

Peterborough projects

The profiles which follow include two women's groups based in schools, a men's forum based at the Peterborough Centre for Multicultural Education and a family literacy project which was run on a split site basis, in a primary school and at the Peterborough Centre for Multicultural Education.

Women's groups

Setting up

The women's groups were set up in 1993 as joint initiatives between schools and the Cambridgeshire Multicultural Education Service. The two schools were junior schools which were able to link with their adjoining infant feeder schools for this project. Children from minority ethnic groups represent approximately 10 per cent to 20 per cent of the school population in both cases.

Listening to parents

Several mothers had approached Section 11 staff informally and expressed a desire to improve their English, through setting up a class based at the school.

After discussions with the headteacher of each school, it was agreed that setting up a women's group might be a start to meeting the parents' needs and involving them more in the life of the school.

Home visits

Section 11 teachers and bilingual assistants working in the schools carried out home visits to all bilingual mothers in both schools to ascertain the level of interest and motivation of the women, as well as get an idea of a possible focus for the group. The 'home visit form' was talked through and completed with the parents. Information collected this way was then communicated to the headteachers who supported the initiative by providing a venue and funding. In both cases the schools agreed to fund the initiative jointly, providing money for refreshments. It was agreed that a Section 11 teacher and a bilingual assistant could staff the group. In one school the headteacher released a mainstream early years teacher for a term to attend the group. One group was held in the dining hall, which had access to a cooking area, complete with sink, fridge, cooker and microwave, and the other in a spare classroom with a sink. Both schools provided toys for the preschool children to use and facilities for hot drinks.

The sessions

The women attending the groups (between five and ten regular attenders) are from different religious backgrounds, Muslim, Sikh and Hindu, and speak a range of languages including Urdu, Punjabi, Gujerati and Bengali. The sessions are always a result of negotiation and consultation involving the Section 11 staff, the women and the headteachers.

Each session has a theme, which is agreed by the women themselves. Sometimes this is developed by an outside speaker, but on occasions, group members lead the session by sharing their own skills and expertise, e.g. sewing skills (cutting and sewing shalwar kameez), cooking skills (preparing samosas) and artistic skills (demonstration of mendhi patterns). This approach has enabled the women to become more self-assured and maintain ownership of the group. Where input is organised by teachers, discussion is encouraged by using collaborative activities. This approach is especially useful in the sessions for English improvement. Usually there is a break in the middle of the session for refreshments which provides an opportunity for informal conversation.

The preschool-age children who attend the group with their mothers are a shared responsibility of the staff running the group. Attendance has remained fairly consistent, with between five and ten women participating.

Support is provided by the Cambridgeshire Multicultural Education Service, through Section 11 teachers and bilingual assistants, with additional input being given by home–school liaison officers. More recently, further support has been given by community education who have provided ESOL tutors. In order to prevent the women's groups from being viewed as a peripheral Section 11 initiative mainstream teachers are encouraged to get involved.

Measurable outcomes

As a result of the groups women have since felt able and valued in the classroom context and have participated in assemblies. Class teachers have sought the advice of the women on the appropriateness of content for assemblies covering other religious festivals such as Eid, Diwali and Narvartri. In one school, one of the women worked with a group of children of different backgrounds for half a term on a weekly basis to teach them a stick dance which was performed at a Year 5 celebration concert.Women from the group also worked with some children at lunchtimes to support them with their computer skills. Apart from working in the classroom, women have also given cooking demonstrations at coffee mornings in school, which led to the development of a 'Community Recipe Book'.

General

The benefits of the women's groups have been felt by all parties. Greater parental involvement in school activities has been noted.

Representatives from the groups have attended training in how to make a video. As a result of this training, a video has been produced about women's groups which has subsequently been used for governor training. At one school, five regular attendees of the women's group were encouraged by the Section 11 teacher to join a family literacy project held in school. One woman who attends the women's group has since become a bilingual assistant and one woman is now taking an RSA First Certificate English course at the Peterborough Regional College.

Finally, staff involved in working with the groups have gained valuable experience which they have disseminated to other Section 11 and mainstream staff, both formally and informally. In-service training has been delivered, both as part of an induction programme to newly appointed Section 11 staff and at a county conference for the Cambridgeshire Multicultural Education Service. As a result, colleagues have gone on to set up groups in other schools.

The men's forum

Identifying the needs

One of the home–school liaison officers based in Peterborough found that his professional role of linking families with schools led naturally into the establishment of this group. As a Muslim who has come through the British educational system himself, as well as working as a bilingual assistant in a Peterborough school, he represented an obvious link between the community and schools. Although women's groups have been a recognised part of school and community development for some time, it became clear that

136

similar groups could be beneficial for men. The home visits carried out during the course of the home–school liaison officer brief, e.g. for admissions and exclusions revealed that many fathers from minority ethnic communities felt alienated from the education system and therefore ill equipped to deal with situations as they arose. Some of the reasons for this were cited as:

- lack of confidence in using English sufficiently well to communicate concerns and desires;
- no knowledge of the system as they were not educated in England;
- limited knowledge of whom to contact for support.

These concerns were echoed in informal contacts as well the formalised Mosque meetings and committee meetings for community groups. There was a general feeling of anxiety that parents, especially men, were not able to guide their children through school.

Establishing a group

The home–school liaison officer canvassed opinion from the men in the local community and after about four weeks of research it was agreed that a men's forum should be established. Since the members of the organisations consulted consisted only of men, the single gender nature of the group was discussed. The men agreed that they would feel more comfortable in an all male group, co-ordinated by men. The men who responded positively to the idea were all from the Pakistani community in the immediate vicinity of the Peterborough Centre for Multicultural Education. However, many children from this community attend secondary schools in outlying areas. It was agreed, therefore, that a group could be set up at the Centre, meeting regularly once a week for two hours.

The sessions

The group consists of eight men who attend regularly. At the outset, the men decided that they would like to split the session in two, having the first hour as an English improver's course taught by a male qualified teacher, and the second hour dedicated to an informal discussion or for an invited speaker. Community education provided a male tutor for the English classes. The men in the group were at different levels of literacy in English: some of the men had recently arrived in England from Pakistan, with good literacy skills in English but in need of extra support for their spoken English. Others well established in Britain were competent speakers of English but needed support in reading and writing.

Meeting the very mixed needs of the group necessitated differentiated materials and a variety of teaching methods and approaches. The home–school liaison officer worked with the ESOL tutor to develop appropriate multicultural resources and participative activities to promote learning and boost confidence and providing language support in Punjabi and Urdu wherever necessary. Guest speakers have come from a range of backgrounds to talk about different aspects of education.

Outcomes

The men attending the forum are taking a more active role in their children's education, attending parents' evenings and PTA meetings as well as attending governor training.

The most obvious benefit of the men's forum has been the increased confidence of the men. This has manifested itself in their take up of further education and courses for their own professional development, e.g. GCSEs. There have also been benefits to the multicultural education service in that we are now better placed to meet the needs of the local community, another channel of communication is open to us and the subsequent links between the community and the school have been strengthened.

Gladstone family literacy project

Background

The Gladstone catchment area is composed almost entirely of Muslim Punjabi-speaking families. Children from the families in this area bring language experiences and skills to school which add richly to their learning. They are expected to maintain their first (spoken) language Punjabi, as well as the recognised language of literacy, Urdu (spoken and written), Arabic is learned for religious reading, while English is the medium of instruction at school. Children from this community develop an awareness of languages and language use but have very few English-speaking role models at school where 98 per cent of the school composition is made up of children from Punjabi/Urdu speaking backgrounds. Difficulties in literacy and oracy in English were identified as issues to be addressed and the family literacy project was set up as the first step in the process.

ALBSU (now renamed the Basic Skills Agency) provided funding for the project and, although the organisation was not involved at the planning stage, it did require an evaluation and review of the work. The project was set up as a joint initiative between the Cambridgeshire Multicultural Education Service and Gladstone Primary School. It was felt that parents working alongside their children in class would help develop bilingual literacy and pre-literacy skills as well as promote self-esteem and raise achievement. The class-based work and the related theoretical sessions held at the Peterborough Centre for Multicultural Education were planned to help parents to understand the rationale behind good primary practice, and involve them in many aspects of their children's learning.

Setting up

A series of home visits was planned for the new reception intake and Year 1 in September. Families were invited to become involved with the project and information was distributed to the interested families by visits, a letter in English and Urdu and materials relating to the proposed course. Informal meetings with parents were held before and after school as well as during mother and toddler sessions. A pre-course meeting was arranged to set the scene and answer any questions. All initial contacts with parents emphasised the advantages of the course and the importance of commitment.

The project planned to give parents two afternoon sessions in school working with their children with one morning session at the Peterborough Centre for Multicultural Education. The project was planned to run for twelve weeks from October 1994 to February 1995. A wide range of educational and employment experiences was represented in the group.

The family literacy group

There were twelve women involved in the project. The linguistic and academic backgrounds of the women can be summarised as shown in Tables 12.1 and 12.2.

Table 12.1 Academic background

Age range	Numbers	Education	Employment
18–25	3	1 Pakistan 2P and GB	nil
25–30	3	3	2 Home (sewing)
30–45	6	6 Pakistan	1 Part time + 1 sewing

The sessions

The course members showed commitment from day one. Their attendance was excellent and they even elected to work with older children in Years 4, 5 and 6. Once established, the women shaped and developed their role in the classroom beyond our expectations, becoming confident and competent role models for teachers and children alike. The children were keen to work with their parents and teachers commented on improved attitudes and achievement of children working with an adult member of the family. The learning which emerged from this project has paid

Table 12.2 Language skills

Language	Speak	Write	Read
Punjabi	12 Adults, 16 Children	0	0
Urdu	12 Adults, 6 Children	6 Adults, 4 Children	6 Adults, 4 Children
Arabic	0	0	12 Adults, 6 Children (for Quran)
English	6 Adults, 13 Children (2 only a little)	5 Adults, 13 Children	5 Adults, 13 Children

dividends in terms of success and achievement. The course members, aware of the reasons behind classroom practice, were able to develop their own good practice, especially with regard to story telling, reading and using their bilingual skills.

Outcomes

The long-term outcomes of this course have been very positive. The 'pioneer' women have been excellent role models for other parents interested in further projects. Many of the women work in the school on a regular basis now and the academic achievement of their children has noticeably improved. This year's SATS results show that three children (who participated in the project) have achieved higher levels in reading and writing than previously anticipated. Many of the mothers found the project so liberating that they have enrolled in English classes and Access courses. Four have successfully completed the RSA certificate for bilingual staff working in multicultural schools. A new group of mothers has since started working in reception alongside their children, encouraged by the original group of parents. The benefits experienced by the teachers were also remarkable, the following quotations from teachers reinforce the positive value of the project:

- 'I believe that the children who took part made more progress than they would have done had their parents not worked with them.'
- 'There is now a much stronger bond between home and school. Parents understand tasks and the reasons for doing various activities. They can therefore support the children appropriately at home and promote achievement.'

- 'I have seen accelerated progress in the children who took part in the project, especially in terms of literacy in English.'

Ways forward

A school committee has been set up to record parents' work, review and evaluate progress and teachers supporting the project are researching the possibilities of accreditation. It has been recognised by the school and the service that family literacy needs to be built into the school development plan to ensure long-term continuity. Governors, staff and community all have a vital role to play in supporting such initiatives in the future. It is only through developing these long-term partnerships that the sustained benefits of family literacy will take root and become a central pivot of school and community life.

Groups in Cambridge: Mahila Ashar – Chesterton Asian Women's Group

Background

This group met weekly in the community education section of Chesterton Community College and also once a week at another venue where the emphasis of the sessions was on improving the women's English language skills. The meetings at Chesterton were informal and social, designed for them to build upon what they had learnt in English and also as a forum for discussion. It was at these sessions that issues concerning the education of their children were raised and the group expressed their concern about their own children's experiences in school. Although they had been meeting at the college for some time, they had little contact with staff or pupils, merely using the college as a venue. Attendance at parents' evenings and other school functions by Asian parents was limited. Although parents responded to home visits and telephone calls from bilingual staff from the multicultural education service they were reluctant to enter into a dialogue with English-speaking staff at the college.

The women themselves said they felt intimidated by the idea of being consulted by teachers about their children's education and their lack of confidence related not only to their limited English language skills but also to their ignorance of the secondary school system.

The programme

The focus of the group, therefore, was to empower the women to enable them to feel a part of the school community and play a more active part in their children's education. To achieve this, we drew up a programme of activities which would both inform the women and give them practical experience, similar to the pupils attending the college.

Sessions

The programme was planned and delivered by bilingual and teaching staff from the Cambridgeshire Multicultural Education Service and the local community development officer. Between five and ten women attended the sessions, most of whom either already had children at Chesterton or in the feeder primary school. The majority were Bengali-speakers, mostly with a basic knowledge of English. The interpreter was present at each session and she also translated some of the written information, handouts or tasks in advance. The sessions ensured the women gained an insight into school life with some practical experience of the curriculum, as well as contributing to their English language learning in speaking, listening, reading and writing.

Each session offered a different approach to getting to know the school. The quiz 'What happens at Chesterton' was undertaken in small groups, each group had a college prospectus and had to find the information to answer the questions on their worksheet. For this activity they were required to read and write in English but could discuss the information among themselves and with the interpreter in Bengali. The activity also aimed to inform the women about how the college functioned, whom they should contact, what role people had at the college, etc. The session 'Whose responsibility is it?' was designed:

- to engender discussion among the group;
- to find out the women's views.

In most cases, the women came to a consensus that the responsibility lay jointly with school, home and children, thus highlighting the importance of close home–school ties.

Both the science and modern languages lessons were delivered by mainstream teachers and were examples of what Year 7 pupils experience at the college. These were followed by visits to both departments and brief in-class observation. The Resource Centre visit and quiz offered a similar experience and had the added bonus that the women were able to borrow some of the Bengali books from the centre. The IT lesson was especially prepared for them by a member of the department, bearing in mind that they were working in their second language and through a medium entirely new to them. During one session, we visited two work experience placements, where Year 10 pupils were working at the time, and in each venue – a hotel and Texas Homecare – the personnel responsible for the students during their placement talked to the group about the duties the students were expected to undertake and answered questions.

In the course of the term, a number of college staff, including the headteacher, came to talk to the group about a variety of issues including PE and careers. This gave both staff and parents an opportunity to meet on an informal basis, gave the women points of contact within the college and gave the staff involved an insight into the background of a number of their pupils. The final session comprised a tour of the college and visits to lessons where some of their own children were being taught. Having followed the programme outlined, the women, by this stage, had the confidence to go into classes and to speak to both pupils and teachers. Also, the pupils' reaction to the women was noticeably changed. Whereas at first their own children had reacted to their presence in the college with embarrassment and others had displayed obvious curiosity, by the end of term the group had become so familiar to all pupils that they were regarded as a regular feature.

At the end of the programme an evaluation sheet was completed by each member of the group. The results showed that the most popular activities were the practical ones such as the computer lesson and visit to work placements. There was a general consensus that they had learnt a great deal about the workings of the college, the daily routine of its pupils and what was required of their own children.

Outcomes

In the year that followed the programme, the women with children at the college attended parents' evenings and other college functions. They also felt empowered to contact college staff such as heads of year when issues arose. The group still meets for weekly English language lessons at another venue but a change of personnel at the college, both Section 11 staff and community development officer, meant that the meetings at Chesterton are no longer held on a regular basis. However, there are plans to start GCSE Bengali classes at the college, and it is hoped that some of the members of the original group will attend these lessons.

The effects on the pupils whose mothers attended the group were certainly notable in that they showed a marked increase in confidence in class and in school in general. By including the women in the weekly routine of the college, the programme not only empowered them but also showed their children that the college valued their culture, background and experiences.

Successes, shortcomings and future challenges

The indirect but over-riding purpose of formalised parents' groups is to raise the academic achievement of black and bilingual pupils in schools. The Cambridgeshire Multicultural Education Service began with the view that enabling parents to support their children's schoolwork would have a potential pay-off in terms of measurable results that would be significant and permanent.

The combined experience of the parents' groups described in this chapter bears out the premise that this aim is possible if not yet fully realised. Individual children have undoubtedly benefited because their parents have been part of a positive and exciting venture focused on education. Common threads in all the groups have been:

- enjoyment;
- discussion;
- parental participation;
- improvement in parents' skills;
- access to information about education;
- increased levels of self-esteem.

The account of the family literacy project, in particular, demonstrates the contribution that parents have made to individual classes and to the wider community through the formal qualifications that several of its members have gained. The case studies described earlier in this chapter hint at developments that need to take place if current achievements are not to fade away. In order for change to take root and not be reliant on the energy of individual people, three aspects, as yet relatively undeveloped, need to be considered, i.e. autonomy, mainstream impetus, in-service training.

Autonomy

Resourcing a group, in terms of staff time, is expensive. Numbers of participants are, typically, relatively small and staff time has to be taken from other activities. Allocating a member of staff to co-ordinate a group is not cost effective if it is on an indefinite basis. One of the basic aims of each group must be to make it independent and to give its members the confidence and the desire to start new groups. Accreditation can play a key part in this, particularly if it provides career progression for individuals. But there are other ways to ensure a group's continuation after the withdrawal of its original co-ordinator. The men's forum, for example, contains within it two Imams of local mosques as well as representatives of community organisations. If their authority and established networks can be tapped into, then the skills which they bring to the group, allied to their newly acquired knowledge, could be used for wider community development. In these circumstances, support from the Cambridgeshire Multicultural Education Service would continue to be available, but the centre of gravity of the group would have changed.

Mainstream impetus

Initiating and co-ordinating parents' groups can easily be seen by mainstream staff as an activity that is typically the role of Section 11 staff. Many

Section 11 staff themselves feel that it is part of their role and because they enjoy the work, do not want to relinquish it. The danger of this approach is that parents groups could continue to exist on the periphery of school life, an activity that mainstream staff contribute to, but are not part of. In order for the notion of a parents' group to take root within a school and for its purpose to be acknowledged, its development must be part of the school's mainstream School Development Plan, with costs, targets, performance indicators and intended outcomes clearly agreed. Headteachers must be convinced enough of the value of parents' groups to make money and staff time available. The school's involvement must go far beyond simply making a space available for others to meet in. In this respect, Cambridgeshire still has some way to go, not because headteachers are unsympathetic, but because the acceptance of the value of parents' groups, in hard, measurable educational terms related to pupils' achievement, is still at an early stage. The efforts and energy of staff from the Cambridgeshire Multicultural Education Service would be best directed to communicating this, even at the expense of time spent in face-to-face contact with parents.

In-service training

In order for mainstream staff to have ownership of the development of parents' groups as an effective route to pupil achievement, they need:

- access to high quality in-service training;
- the motivation to seek out the training for themselves.

Our experience in Cambridgeshire is that a number of staff have become enthusiastic about the value of parents' groups, but that it is difficult to break into the realm of providing training for all. The Cambridgeshire Multicultural Education Service holds staff meetings in schools and provides a very comprehensive range of in-service workshops and courses, including some on setting up and co-ordinating parents' groups.

Convincing headteachers and schools' in-service co-ordinators that this is an area of development that should be given priority over other pressing areas is a challenge, but persuading them that it is so effective in terms of results that it is worth taking staff out of classrooms is another. Both these challenges need to be met if the wider benefits that can flow from well-run individual projects are to permeate the system and really make a permanent difference.

13 Working towards partnership: parents, teachers and community organisations

Raymonde Sneddon

Introduction

When my child started school he cried in the morning and clung to my hand as I tried to leave him at the classroom door. I became a teacher because I was invited to come in and sit on the mat with him. I listened to the morning story and slipped away when he had settled. Some time later when he said 'I wish you could come and see me do my work' I was invited to spend a day in the school. In the course of that day I was initiated in the mysteries of the sentence maker, of the extraordinarily complex planning behind the successfully rotating group work and of the staff room at lunch. I marvelled at the skill displayed in class by the young teacher and I wondered 'Could I...?'

When my other child started in a special school and I was trying to come to terms with his disability the headteacher offered tea, sympathy and tissues in abundance. She also offered 'Come and spend a day in school every week'. It was a moment of great pride when my child took my hand, led me to his table and said wordlessly 'Come and see me do my work'.

As a parent and a long-standing community activist, when I did become a teacher it seemed self-evident that these positive experiences should be the right of all parents. I also became aware that my early experiences of education had been unusual. In the course of my work as a teacher I met .colleagues, community activists and parents who helped me to understand how trust could be built.

Home–school liaison in multilingual schools: some perceived problems

Since the publication of the Plowden Report in 1967, primary schools have been encouraged to develop and strengthen their links with parents and the community. Schools have moved progressively from providing regular school reports and open evenings, to sending regular letters home, to promoting parent–teacher associations and organising social events and meetings to explain teaching methods. Many schools ask parents to help as volunteers to support school outings, hear children read and assist in practical activities.

The findings of the Haringey research (Tizard *et al.* 1982) encouraged many schools to promote home–school reading partnerships and some schools went to great lengths to encourage the involvement of as many parents as possible. However, it is still the case that in most schools only a minority of parents are actively involved in their children's education. Schools regularly complain that certain parents never come to school and that all their initiative has only reinforced the participation of those who are already involved. Mythologies spring up in staff rooms about certain categories of parent who are 'not interested in education'. Many schools find the task of involving parents who may not be fluent in English daunting and have resigned themselves to low levels of participation.

Barriers to communication

The cultural and linguistic distance between homes and school has been well documented. In the home children use language to communicate and discuss everyday matters in a context that is supportive of their meaning (Wells 1986, Tizard and Hughes 1984). In the world of the classroom language is used differently. The opportunities to talk about matters of immediate interest are fewer, ritual display questions abound and much discussion takes place which is removed from an immediate context. Those children who have had experiences of story telling, story reading and problem-solving discussions in the home will find the gap somewhat less daunting than others.

The home–school reading schemes used in many schools have helped to bridge that gap. Even when no quantifiable improvement in reading has been recorded as a result of these programmes, schools have reported that improved relationships with families and a sense of common purpose have been beneficial to children's education. However, schools have expressed concern that, in most cases, these schemes reinforce the advantage that children have who come from homes that are literate in English. Only a school very committed to the development of all its children explores ways in which parents who are anxious about their own levels of literacy and those for whom English is not the language of the home can best support their children.

Research since the 1960s has shown that bilingualism is not a cognitive handicap, need not be an educational one and, in favourable circumstances, can be a considerable intellectual and educational asset (Cummins 1984). Where the first language of a child is valued in society and well established for both communication and literacy, acquisition of a second language is likely to be successful. The knowledge of literacy and of language usage out of context that a child has acquired in her first language will transfer and facilitate that child's acquisition of literacy in an additional language.

However, the key to successful bilingualism lies in the relative status and power of linguistic groups in the community. Where the family's home language is not valued in society, when opportunities for developing the full range of language functions and literacy are few and the goal of education is entirely to develop the second language, the educational outcomes for bilingual children are not favourable. Unsurprisingly, if children are expected to acquire new concepts in a barely familiar language they will experience considerable difficulties. And so will their parents.

The difficulties experienced by parents from the majority culture in communicating with the school are compounded for minority group parents by a number of factors. In many cases parents, and especially mothers, who generally bring young children to school:

- may have few skills in basic communication in English;
- are not familiar with the school system and do not know who to approach about what, or how to arrange appointments;
- have had little experience of being consulted over their child's education and may have little expectation that the school will change any of its procedures to accommodate problems which they may have;
- have become used to very superficial conversations, to smiling and passing on, as interpreters are rarely available;
- may be very anxious about approaching figures of authority and disclosing personal information, based on experience of other government agencies;
- may have only been called to school in the past when their child was in trouble;
- may find letters and noticeboards daunting and they may find personal communication much more inviting;
- may have expectations of education and ways of supporting children at home that are different and may be far from matching the expectations of the school.

This last issue has been well documented in the famous studies of Shirley Brice Heath (1983) and, more recently, in a London context, by Eve Gregory (Gregory and Biarnes 1994). Corson in this context notes that while parents may 'value literacy, they often feel uncomfortable with the behaviours that the school sees as necessary for its acquisition' (Corson 1993). He further adds that 'if minority children are to take literacy up successfully, the way that schools introduce it and develop it needs to complement rather than threaten to eliminate the life styles that rightly have high cultural value' (Corson 1993).

Issues of power

Schools are inclined to forget what daunting places they are to many parents. They also give out very mixed messages. On my first visit to a school in my role as a teacher educator I recently had a long conversation with a headteacher who bemoaned the fact that 'parents in this area are not interested in education' and that her efforts to involve parents had met with slender success. As I left the school I stepped over the tell-tale white line in the playground that proclaimed 'no parents beyond this point'. How long had it been there? Did the headteacher remember its existence? Was she aware of the contradiction? On what terms was she trying to involve parents?

In his analysis of the relationship between minority communities and schools, Cummins notes the institution's assumption that:

> since equality of opportunity is believed to be a given, it is assumed that individuals are responsible for their own failure and are, therefore, made to feel that they have failed because of their own inferiority, despite the best efforts of dominant-group institutions and individuals to help them.
>
> (Cummins 1986)

Cummins suggests a four-point model to promote educational success for linguistic minority students. It includes actively involving minority languages and culture within the school, developing an interactive teaching style that promotes the acquisition of English in a meaningful and supportive context, assessment procedures that acknowledge the full range of children's experiences and the context of their learning and, crucially, the participation of communities in the schooling process. 'When educators value minority parents as partners in their children's education, parents appear to develop a sense of efficacy that communicates itself to children, with positive academic consequences' (Cummins 1986).

Models of partnership between schools and minority communities can be found around the world. Some outstanding examples are available from New-Zealand, Australia, Canada and California (Corson 1993). All of these are based on the concept that an effective partnership has to empower a local community.

How this partnership can be achieved is described by Faltis (1993). His model of 'joinfostering' developed in Californian schools that cater for a majority of Spanish-speaking children has much that can be transferred to the English educational context. It requires teachers to move out of the classroom and into the community. Faltis notes that parents are unlikely, as in the school referred to above, to become involved in the school simply because the headteacher wants them to. Successful partnership requires teachers to 'strike a balance between learning about the home environment of [their] students while the parents … learn about school-oriented activities' (Faltis 1993).

He proposes a four-level approach to partnership development:

- the teacher learns about the community, initiating individual contact with parents and jointly monitoring children's progress in school;
- information is shared with parents on a wide range of school and community issues, using both letters and personal communication;
- parents are invited to participate both formally and informally in activities in the classroom and the school;
- the final level is referred to as the 'empowerment' level. It involves encouraging parents who may be interested to take part in the formal decision-making process of the school (i.e. as governors).

This approach is reflected in the work of David Corson (1993) who stresses that successful partnerships are based on meeting community needs at the level of the school and its immediate catchment area.

Bridging the gap

Research carried out among 50 bilingual families in a northeast London borough (Sneddon 1994) revealed the following:

- in few cases was an interpreter other than the child available to facilitate communication at parents' meetings;
- parents meetings were often inflexible in their timing, making it difficult for parents with work or family commitments to attend. Parents felt unable to communicate this to the school and were concerned about being considered to be 'not interested' in their child's education;
- teachers lacked awareness of the languages used by a family for communication and literacy and showed little interest in children's achievements in these.

It has been suggested that attendance at parents' evenings should be made compulsory. Before such extreme (and counter-productive) methods are adopted, schools need to consider the following:

- is the school environment genuinely welcoming to parents who may be unfamiliar with both the language and the conventions of the school?
- are parents' and children's linguistic skills and religious requirements acknowledged and respected as of right?
- are parents from all communities consulted about the timing and type of events, taking into account family, work and religious commitments as well as the dangers of coming out after dark in certain areas?
- are events publicised in an appropriate manner: by letter in the right language or through oral communication?
- is supervision provided for younger children?
- are initiatives taken, depending on a school's staffing and space resources, to encourage active partnership e.g. parents' rooms, home–school visiting, classes or advice surgeries on school premises?

In a multilingual school a teacher recently arranged for interpreters to be available for all parents who needed them. Letters were sent home. The interpreters telephoned the families who did not respond to these and invited them personally to the school at a mutually convenient time. All parents contacted attended, many for the first time. Once the initial contact was made and the ice was broken parents found visiting school far less daunting and special measures were not required for many of those parents in the long term.

The role of the community organisation

In the context of the models of participation described above, which require teachers to step outside their classrooms and get to know their communities, community organisations can provide a crucial link and a starting point.

Exploring new partnerships: some examples

Working with the Turkish Education Group

In the process of monitoring the children's performance and learning to reach out to its community, a school (in which 62 per cent of children were bilingual in a range of 20 languages) found that a group of Turkish-speaking children were underachieving significantly. It was further noted that their parents very rarely came to school in spite of letters having been sent home in Turkish. A group which specialised in providing educational support to the Turkish community was approached for advice.

An educational consultant from the group came to visit the school. She met with the head and concerned teachers and recommended that the head call a consultative meeting of all Turkish-speaking parents. She wrote the letter of invitation which indicated to parents that their views on the education of their children were being sought and that she would personally attend as interpreter and advocate. Much to the surprise of the school all families were represented.

The meeting was given a very high priority by the headteacher. It was held during school time, in a specially prepared room with refreshments available. The first part of the meeting was planned to raise general issues with all parents. For the second part alterations had been made to the school timetable to enable all concerned class teachers to come and meet the parents.

Some of the parents who attended spoke little English, none was knowledgeable about the English education system and all wondered why they had been asked. The educational consultant acted not only as a translator of language, but, very importantly, also as a translator of expectation. Her skills enabled teachers to explain that to educate the children successfully they needed to know about their linguistic and cultural background and that the best people to provide this were the parents themselves. Most importantly those parents were able to tell the teachers about their expectations of the school and their aspirations for their children.

As the meeting progressed it became obvious that parents had a wide range of concerns about their children's schooling but had never felt able to discuss these, partly because of the language barrier and partly because they were unsure of what the school's response would be. Individual concerns raised included the following:

- a child frequently absent from school because of bullying;

- a child regularly left after school because his mother had to wait for the school bus to bring home another child from a special school;
- concerns from a number of parents about the diet available for Muslim children at lunchtime;
- concerns about the procedure for assessing children's special educational needs;
- the timing of parents' evenings;
- the provision of homework (including reading);
- the availability of extra English support for children who needed it in class;
- the availability of Turkish classes for children in the community.

At the end of the meeting an action plan was drawn up to address all of these issues, including dates by which the school would report back to parents on progress. Parents were able to meet their children's teacher and to discuss progress with the help of the educational consultant. Where a further meeting was required this was arranged so that an interpreter could be present. Some parents raised problems regarding housing and social services with the consultant who was able to direct them to appropriate help within the community.

In the short term the school had learned about many issues that affected the learning of the children and the parents had learned that they could raise issues with the school which would be addressed. In the long term the ice had been broken: communication had been established and it was maintained to the measurable benefit of the children concerned. One mother came and joined the school's mother-and-child writing group and two came together to the adult education English classes that were run on school premises at that time. Two children were enrolled at Turkish classes run by the community group and all were made aware of the facilities offered by the group to families. In addition the consultant invited teachers to visit the group's offices, provided information on education in Turkey and advised on the selection of suitable children's books in Turkish for the school library.

Working with the Asian Women's Support Group

Some two years later teachers at the same school became concerned about a group of Sylheti-speaking children. Like the previously noted group the children were noticeably underachieving educationally but they also seemed more isolated within the school and more economically deprived than most of the school population. Most of them had recently arrived in the area and some were living in temporary accommodation in very unsuitable premises. There was no established Bengali community in the immediate area and none of the families had close relatives or friends near by. In spite of considerable classroom help from language support teachers the children were not progressing. The women who brought the children to school spoke no English and did not respond to letters sent home.

Hoping to repeat the success of the previous strategy, the school approached a voluntary organisation which supports Asian women. The group sent representatives to the school to meet the teachers and discuss their concerns. They contacted the mothers of the children concerned personally and held a private meeting with them on school premises. Again the school were surprised by the high attendance. This meeting was followed by a general meeting of all the school teachers, with the women and the three advocates from the support group. At this meeting the advocates outlined requests from the women regarding the education of their children. In addition to meeting with their children's class teachers to discuss their concerns over their children the women were anxious to obtain the help of the school to set up their own support network and they requested in particular a Bengali language class for their children and a regular health and education class for themselves.

From the extensive meetings that took place on that day the teachers discovered much that dismayed them: that many of the families had suffered racist attacks, that the children were being bullied, sometimes on school premises, but more often on the way home.

The experience and the community knowledge of the women's support group provided the key to opening up and resolving these issues which were negatively affecting the children's learning.

Following on the women's request a small self-help group was set up. It was run by a committee which included some of the women concerned, representatives of the support group and school staff. It succeeded in attracting charitable funding. To date, it has been running a Saturday Bengali class for 40 children and a fortnightly women's health education group for six years, to the great educational and social benefit of the children and their families (Sneddon 1993).

What community organisations are and what they do

Inner-city areas with diverse populations generally have a wide range of voluntary organisations that provide support for cultural, linguistic and religious groups. These fulfil a multiplicity of functions such as providing supplementary or language classes, health information and advice, general counselling, employment training, specific support for women, childcare, housing advice and provision, leisure, artistic and sporting facilities, youth clubs, religious services, advice and support for refugees, etc. These organisations vary in size from the small playgroup in someone's front room to the major foundation, run as a limited company with extensive offices, which provides a 'cradle to grave' service for a particular community.

Some organisations provide a wide range of services for a particular linguistic or national group (Chinese or Bangladeshi community centres, for example), others focus on a specific facility for a wider group (Asian Women's

Support group, homework club for Asian students, etc.). The organisations are generally run by volunteer management groups and, when funding permits, some employ paid workers depending on their size and the availability of funding. They are funded from a variety of sources: contributions from the community they serve, local authority grants, grants from major charitable and religious foundations, fees charged for certain services, etc.

Cultural and linguistic networks

The work of anthropologists and sociolinguists like Milroy (1987) has enabled us to understand the role of social networks in maintaining linguistic and cultural buoyancy in a community. Language and culture are strengthened where people can use them in a wide range of domains, such as family life, education, the work place and leisure ('dense' networks) and even more so when these contacts in the network also know each other ('multiplex' networks).

A 'chicken and egg' situation is created: where substantial numbers of members of a particular cultural and linguistic community live close together, they will support each other informally. Community activists may then emerge who will create organisations to meet particular needs within the community. The existence of these organisations, by extending the range of domains in which people can meet, will support the development of increasingly dense and multiplex networks. The strength of these networks and the support they provide for their community will then encourage more people from the community to move into the area.

The skills community organisations can offer

Most of these organisations have developed through local need. In the absence of any national policy for supporting bilingual education they have been almost solely responsible for providing first language education for bilingual children. This important role was documented in the Linguistic Minorities Report (Stubbs 1985). The Swann Report (DES 1985), which failed to support first language education in the state school system for bilingual children, recommended that these organisations be supported by local authorities to provide language classes, through free access to educational premises and various grants. The organisations are the focus for intense community activity, as they attempt to bridge the cultural and linguistic gap and help new minorities both to adapt to life in British society and to maintain a linguistic and cultural identity. They often play a very important part in children's lives of which teachers are completely unaware. Fishman has noted the importance of these groups in promoting minority language interests and in slowing down or reversing minority language loss (Fishman 1990).

Voluntary organisations are not usually funded generously enough to be able to provide a free interpretation and translation service to schools and this should not be expected. However, they are generally keen to establish links with schools and many welcome visits from teachers. They will often be willing to provide information on a particular community, on religious and cultural practices, dietary and health requirements, expectations of education and the history of a particular community. They may also have a particular brief to support individuals in their community who have dealings with educational establishments providing, for example, an advocate to accompany a parent involved in the statementing of a child, exclusion procedures, or an appeal about a school placement. In some cases they are able to provide staff who will come into school to help celebrate festivals, organise a special event, or even organise language classes on a regular basis.

For teachers keen to get to know the community in which they work and the influences that are important in their children's lives community organisations are an invaluable source of information. Those teachers who are not familiar with the locality can often identify organisations close to the school by simply asking the children. Education departments, town halls or libraries may keep a register of voluntary organisations. In some boroughs voluntary groups have formed themselves into an umbrella organisation which will provide a directory (for example, Hackney Community Action).

Educating teachers and schools

Established voluntary and community organisations can play an important part in helping a school to understand and reach out to its community and begin the journey described above with reference to the work of Cummins, Faltis and Corson, referred to earlier. By providing the school with information and advice such organisations are a vital source of education for teachers in a multicultural society. In turn they can benefit from and pass on to parents information about how the school works so that a community of purpose can develop. By acting as go-between in the manner described above the organisations can break down barriers, help establish a triangular parent–school–community network of support and help the school to build a lasting trust with its community.

The above strategies have enabled me as a teacher to waylay mothers who passed with a smile and a 'I don't speak English'. Many have come in to see their child 'do their work'. Some came back week after week and told stories and made books. Some sought educational advice and proceeded to become nursery nurses; for some the involvement and commitment with education grew till they fulfilled the fourth level of Faltis' model and became school governors.

References

Brice Heath, S. (1983) *Ways With Words: ethnography of communication in communities and classrooms.* Cambridge: Cambridge University Press.

Corson, D. (1993) *Language, Minority Education and Gender: linking social justice and power.* Clevedon: Multilingual Matters.

Cummins, J. (1984) *Bilingualism and Special Education: issues in assessment and pedagogy.* Clevedon: Multilingual Matters.

Cummins, J. (1986) 'Empowering Minority Students: a framework for intervention', *Harvard Educational Review*, 56, 1, pp.18–36.

DES (1985) *Education for all.* London: HMSO.

Faltis, C. (1993) 'Building Bridges Between Parents and the School', in Garcia, O. and Baker, C. (Eds) (1995) *Policy and Practice in Bilingual Education: extending the foundations.* Clevedon: Multilingual Matters.

Fishman, J. (1990) 'What is Reversing Language Shift (RLS) and How Can it Succeed?', *Journal of Multilingual and Multicultural Development*, 11, pp.5–36.

Gregory, E. and Biarnes, J. (1994). 'Tony and Jean–Francois looking for sense in the strangeness of school', in Dombey, H. and Meek Spencer, M. (Eds) *First Steps Together: home–school early literacy in European contexts.* Stoke-on-Trent: Trentham Books/IEDPE.

Milroy, L. (1987), *Language and Social Networks.* Oxford: Blackwell.

Sneddon, R. (1993) 'Beyond the National Curriculum: a community project to support bilingualism', *Journal of Multilingual and Multicultural Development*, 14, 3, pp.237–46.

Sneddon, R. (1994) 'Supporting Children's Literacies at Home', *Language Matters*, 1.

Stubbs, M. (Ed.) (1985) *The Other Languages of England: the Linguistic Minorities Report.* London: Routledge and Kegan Paul.

Tizard, B. and Hughes, M. (1984) *Young Children Learning.* London: Fontana.

Tizard, J., Schofield, W.N. and Hewison, J. (1982) 'Collaboration Between Teachers and Parents in Assisting Children's Reading', *British Psychological Society*, 52,1, pp.1–15.

Wells, G. (1986) *The Meaning Makers.* London: Hodder and Stoughton.

Index

Note: Underlined numbers indicate tables.